D1064608

mind-blowing
sex

PAUL SCOTT

illustrations by pinglet@pvuk.com

RYLAND
PETERS
& SMALL

LONDON NEW YORK

Senior Designer **Paul Tilby**
Editor **Miriam Hyslop**
Production **Gavin Bradshaw**
Art Director **Gabriella Le Grazie**
Publishing Director **Alison Starling**

Illustrations **pinglet@pvuk.com**

First published in the
United States in 2005
by Ryland Peters & Small, Inc.
519 Broadway
5th Floor
New York NY 10012
www.rylandpeters.com

10 9 8 7 6 5 4 3 2 1

Text, design, and illustrations
© Ryland Peters & Small 2005

All rights reserved. No part of this publication may
be reproduced, stored in a retrieval system, or
transmitted in any form or by any means, electronic,
mechanical, photocopying, or otherwise, without
the prior permission of the publisher.

Library of Congress Cataloging-in-Publication Data

Scott, Paul, 1965-
  Mind-blowing sex / by Paul Scott.
     p. cm.
  Includes index.
  ISBN 1-84172-788-1
  1. Sex instruction. 2. Sex. I. Title.
  HQ31.S465 2005
  613.9'6–dc22

                                    2004020836

Printed in China

It is the reader's responsibility to abide by the laws
of their territory of residence. Neither the author nor
the publisher can be held responsible or liable for
any claim arising out of the use, or misuse of the
information or advice contained in this book.

contents

introduction

Informative, accessible, and packed with exciting tips and tricks that are guaranteed to arouse, *Mind-blowing Sex* takes a light-hearted approach to lovemaking, and will encourage you and your partner to explore your sexuality.

Once upon a time, sex manuals had to be earnest, dry, and full of diagramatic line drawings in order to prove that they were respectable and sincere. These days we understand that just because something's about sex, that doesn't make it pornography. This book is a full, frank, and helpful guide to getting the most out of your sexual self.

We would probably agree that for us all, whether we're just getting to know our partners or have been together long-term, there is always room for improvement; always something we didn't know, which is bound to turn us on. Exploring everything from sexy massage to sex toys, from arousal to "afterplay", *Mind-blowing Sex* covers a range of diverse subjects as well as putting a sexy new spin on the ones we know and love.

Improving your sex life isn't just a physical matter—this book is about how to relax with your partner. There is no obligation to have great sex—do it because you want to! Not feeling pressured is essential to having fun. Arousal is a state of mind in which the possibilities seem endless. So settle back, make yourself comfortable, and, with the aid of this book, be inspired to think of the exciting new directions your bedroom play could take!

for starters

Whether you're in a long-term relationship,

or are with someone with whom you are experiencing the pleasures of

lovemaking for the first time, there will be a host of new ways to excite

your lover, and a range of sexual avenues that neither of you will have

explored. There's no substitute sometimes for going back to basics,

and thinking afresh about what your lover might enjoy...

on the brain

The awakening of sexual arousal, as we all know, triggers physical changes. Humankind has puzzled for centuries about how thought becomes action, and it is now believed to take place in a part of the brain called the limbic system. When you perceive something as sexy, changes to the body begin in this part of the brain. The perceptions of touch, taste, and smell are interpreted here, as are your thoughts, desires, and fantasies.

The limbic system converts what is on our minds into physical feelings. In the case of sexual desire, the message being sent out by the brain is to increase blood flow to the genitals, and this is known as psychogenic arousal. The limbic system is complex, mysterious, and not completely understood. Just as we can experience symptoms of stress for which we don't know the immediate cause, so too we can experience the sensations of sexual arousal without there being an obvious cause present. Thoughts, alone, are powerful drives.

Of course, sexual desire can also be sparked by something purely physical—anything from an erotic massage to direct genital manipulation can get our pulses racing and our juices flowing. This is called reflex arousal, and is far simpler but less common than psychogenic arousal.

During lovemaking, reflex and psychogenic arousal work together to create the physical symptoms of desire. You can be doing all the right things physically and your partner may still not be sufficiently aroused if there's no psychological stimulus, or if there's a psychological pressure to show they're having fun. Women and men are complex creatures, and it helps to be patient, not only with your partner, but with yourself.

When we orgasm, we release endorphins—the "happy hormones" that flood through our veins when we're on a roller-coaster, or in love. It is these hormones that give us that buzz of pleasure.

her pleasure zones

While male orgasm is improved by all-over body contact and skin-on-skin stimulation, women, in general, need it if they are to come at all. Many women, too, say that how they are touched is as important as where. If in doubt, imagine it is you who is being touched the way that you are touching your partner—would you like what you are doing?

Apart from her genitals, here are ten areas that can be almost as thrilling:

Mouth

Bottom

Breasts and nipples

Hands, arms, and armpits

Face and scalp

Back of the neck and ear lobes

Shoulders

Feet, backs of knees, and inner thighs

Back

Tummy

his pleasure zones

Men's bodies are incredibly sensitive and are full of concentrated nerve-endings in places other than the obvious one. Despite what he knows he likes, he may not be aware of what an all-over-body experience sex could be for him.

His ten thrilling places:

Mouth

Buttocks and anus

Chest and nipples

Hands and inside the elbows

Scalp and hairline

Ear lobes and inside the ear

Neck and shoulders

Feet

Small of the back

Tummy

her genitals

There are as many different sets of female genitals as there are women. Female biology includes many variations, all of which are normal.

Clitoris Nowhere else in the human body—male or female—are there so many sensitive nerve endings packed into such a small space. You can find the clitoris under a tiny hood—the prepuce—at the top of the vulva. The only visible part is the tip, which looks like a tiny pinkish bud—but the blood vessels and nerve endings attached to it go back far into the tummy.

Vulva There are two sets of labia which, together with the clitoris, make up the vulva (the externally visible bits).

The outer and inner lips The labia majora, or outer lips, are fleshy folds of skin, hairy on the outside and with sweat glands on the inside. They vary wildly in shape and size from woman to woman, depending on age and ethnicity. Just inside these are the labia minora—hairless folds of skin that extend from the clitoral hood to the back of the vulva. In some women, the labia minora are tucked inside the labia majora, while in others the inner lips protrude beyond the outer ones. It is here that a woman's individual sexual smell is secreted.

Vagina This long, muscular, prehensile tube sheathes the penis during intercourse. It is an average of 3½ in. (9 cm) long in its resting state, but, since it can accommodate a baby, it is more than flexible enough to accommodate any penis. The vagina is most sensitive near the opening. The contracting and expanding tissues of the vaginal wall secrete lubricating, viscous vaginal fluid.

Cervix The neck of the womb where the vagina joins the uterus.

Hymen This thin membrane of skin covers the opening of the vagina in very young women and is naturally long gone in most adults. In some cultures, an intact hymen is regarded as evidence of virginity, despite the fact that it is easily broken in many other non-sexual ways. In itself, this vestigial piece of skin has no biological importance. Unbroken, it has a tiny opening to let vaginal secretions and menstrual blood through, and can bleed when it's ruptured.

Perineum The tough, pliant skin between the anus and vagina. It is often overlooked as a place worth stimulating, which is a shame, as it's packed with nerve endings.

G-spot A highly erogenous zone located on the front wall of the vagina. This mass of nerve tissue can't be felt unless it is stimulated. Lots of women say that stimulation on the front of the vaginal wall does nothing for them, others have the orgasms to prove that the G-spot exists.

his genitals

The "standard-issue" penis doesn't exist; the organ varies wildly in shape, size, and color from man to man. They're all made up of the same parts, however.

Urethra The duct that runs up the center of the shaft, carrying urine and semen to the tip of the penis. The skin here is very thin and sensitive and is packed with nerve endings. The average penis measures between 2½–4 in. (6½–10cm) when flaccid, and 6–7 in. (15–18 cm) when erect. Contrary to popular belief, you cannot predict penis size from a man's height, or from the size of his nose, hands, or feet.

Foreskin The head of an uncircumcised penis is covered in a protective layer of loose skin called the foreskin, which wrinkles up when the penis is flaccid. When the penis is erect, the foreskin retracts to expose the glans. The inner surface of the foreskin produces a natural mucus called smegma. Circumcision is the surgical removal of the foreskin. Although performed for cultural as well as medical reasons, there is absolutely no scientific evidence that circumcision is of any benefit whatsoever: it has not been found to increase sensation, and good personal hygiene is sufficient to keep a healthy penis clean. Its widespread use in the USA dates from the nineteenth-century attempt to control the imagined illness of "masturbatory insanity."

Glans The smooth, curved head of the penis has a higher concentration of nerve endings than the shaft, making it the most erogenous area of the male body.

Frenulum The foreskin is attached to the glans by a tiny triangle of super-sensitive skin on the underside of the penis, called the frenulum. It is the most sensitive spot on a man's body, and just a tiny lick here could send him over the edge into orgasm.

Perineum The skin between the scrotum and the anus.

Prostate gland One of nature's better-kept secrets is that anal sex is potentially more rewarding for men than for women. This is because of the sensitive prostate gland, located inside the anus and ¾–1¾ in. (2–4 cm) towards the front, which produces the fluid in which sperm are kept in suspension. If you are not keen on the idea of penetrating him with a strap-on, then the area can usually be reached by digital manipulation, while external pressure on the perineum also stimulates it. His perineum will warm to a loving touch for its own sake, too, as much as a woman's.

Testicles Designed to manufacture sperm and testosterone, the testicles hang loosely behind the penis, encased in the scrotum. It is normal for one testicle to hang lower than the other, so that they are not squeezed when their owner walks and runs. The wrinkly line that runs between the balls, known as the raphe, is another highly sensitive line to trace with the tip of your tongue.

fun flirting

The most effective path to psychogenic arousal is a good old flirt! Don't be nervous—flirting is one of the most enjoyable parts of dating, and puts the excitement back into long-term relationships, too. Even if we're not aware of it, we all use body language, sending out messages that show we're interested in someone. Being aware of what you are saying with your body is as important as what comes out of your mouth.

Where to put your arms Pinning them to your sides sends out a forbidding message, while showing the insides of your wrists signifies approachability. Arms are one of the main areas in which gender differences are visible—soft and feminine, or veined, strong, and manly. Draw attention to your arms with accessories such as bracelets, or with a chunky watch if you're a man.

Showing some leg We tend to point our feet towards someone we're interested in. Stroking their thigh will suggest to your partner that they could do the same and, if you're a woman, you might dangle your shoe seductively on your toes.

Face to face If a person mirrors your body language, it shows they're interested. Face the person with your torso.

On your shoulders Women find broad shoulders attractive in men, so men can try sitting with their shoulders back, which also signifies approachability. Meanwhile, women's shoulders are said to remind men of breasts—smooth and round. Bare shoulders will suggest more.

Flirty hair Playing with your hair mimics how you'd like others to handle you, while hiding behind long hair makes for seductive glances.

In the eyes Candlelight and low lighting make the pupils of our eyes dilate, as they do when we're sexually interested. You might want to stare at your date all night, but it's not very arousing. Hold a gaze for a few seconds and break away. Don't linger and don't focus on one body part—both genders feel uncomfortable with this. Cast an appreciative gaze without staring.

Mouth-to-mouth You're using it to chat, and maybe kiss, so the mouth is an object of attention—lips become redder and more swollen when aroused. Licking and moistening your lips can be sexy so long as it is not overdone.

i just want your extra time and your ... kiss

Despite the amount of social kissing we do, true, deep, erotic kissing remains a form of sex in itself. Sometimes, it is just about the most intimate exchange we can share with someone, more intimate even than intercourse. The lips have the most sensitive skin on the human body, and that's why kissing is the queen of foreplay.

We can be guilty of neglecting kissing if we're in a long-term relationship; when we know a partner's pathways to arousal, we tend to use them first. We may kiss as we go, but it's not the same as necking for a long time, exploring the other person's responses with your kiss, but also treating the kiss as a novelty and an end in itself. Kiss in places other than the bedroom, and not just as foreplay. Kissing is safe, and it is legal in public. So make a point from time to time of kissing for its own sake.

Good dental hygiene will make you a more confident kisser; brushing, flossing, and regular visits to a dentist will stop worries about bad breath preying on your mind. Don't be afraid to be different, passionate and unusual when you kiss; lick, blow, and touch your lover's lips, and don't forget the rest of their face, either. The endorphins you release when you are both aroused raise your pain threshold, turning things that might hurt at other times into pure sensation. So be bold, and don't be afraid to be slightly more aggressive when the kissing is foreplay.

A word in your ear—some people aren't in the least moved by attention to their ears, while others find that a tongue there is guaranteed to hit a motherlode of sexual arousal, and go wild for this noisy, sexy, wet kiss. If they do, make circles with your tongue all over their ear, inside and out. If not, peck your way back to the lips.

Kissing someone's eyes is a gentle, tender, and sometimes surprising favor. Kiss their eyelids gently, with your mouth against the orbit of their eye. Assuming they don't wear contact lenses, it's fine if your tongue touches their eyeball, although they may not appreciate it. In kissing generally, feeling your partner's eyelids flutter, like feeling and tasting their breath, can be a powerfully arousing reminder of your physical closeness.

- Use your fingers. Trace the outline of your lover's lips. You can look into each other's eyes as they get used to the rougher texture of fingers and thumbs.
- Any noises you make will vibrate through your partner's jaw, so if you're given to moaning, don't stop. Show you're aroused and give them a taste of what's to come.
- Gently hold your lover's lower lip between your finger and thumb and roll it, or else take it into your mouth and suck it. The skin of the lower lip gives easily enough for this gesture of pure desire.
- Put your fingers to each other's lips and move them gently in and out of the mouth. It's not surprising that this action is arousing since it mirrors penetration itself.
- Recreate the motions of sex in each other's mouths, especially during intercourse. Slip your tongue between your lover's lips and move it in and out. Simulate the thrusting of the act itself.
- Play with your partner's face as you kiss. Reach up with your fingertips to caress your partner's cheek; take their ears between your thumbs and forefingers, playing gently, and run your hands around the line of their jaw.
- Breathe each other's breath. Make an airtight seal with your lips and inhale deeply.
- Just grazing each other's lips can be intensely arousing—it's an intimate tease. You can also lick and blow on your partner's lips, making their already sensitized surface tingle at the contrast between warm and cool.
- Butterfly kisses are a similarly teasing treat: pepper your partner's face and neck with small, dry kisses from your puckered lips.
- Tickle your partner's palette and gums with your tongue— you'll be saying intimately how much you want them.
- And, of course, when the situation's right, kiss each other all over, and not just around the lips and erogenous zones. Until you've kissed every inch of your lover's body, you can't be sure exactly what effect it may have. Treat the areas your partner likes you to caress to more lingering attention. If you know your hands alone can give pleasure, that's a good reason to find out what your lips can do.

foreplay

undressing each other

- Shirt buttons can be sewn on again.
- Using your teeth to undress your lover is passionate, horny, and practical.
- Alternatively, slow is enticing and arousing. Remove coats and shirts lovingly and seductively. Women, undo a man's belt decisively.
- Men, learn how to undo a bra—don't become trapped in fumbling. One-handed is even better.

foreplay that'll turn him on

Men who think they don't want any foreplay don't know what they've been missing. After experiencing a few of these, they will know it's something to relish in itself.

- If it seems natural, feel him up through his clothes. Not only is it a horny idea, but men's genitals are excited by a range of textures from rough to smooth. You are more likely to touch his most sensitive spots if you cup or grasp them directly from underneath, rather than approaching directly from the front with your hand. This also allows you to press his perineum through his trousers and/or underpants, and to cup and gently roll his balls.
- Gently slapping and tapping his penis in your palm can help to bring it to erection. He may require a firmer touch than yours to get aroused. If you're worried about becoming heavy-handed, though, just ask him to direct you; "harder" or "softer" is all he has to say.
- Caress his chest and thighs with your breasts. Let him feel your nipples. Bring his head into your chest and nuzzle him.
- Hold his penis still while your other hand strokes him elsewhere. The longer you delay penetration, the more ready to come he will be, so holding his penis still will desensitize it, making him last longer.
- With your thumb and index finger forming a tight ring around the base of his penis, press down on his balls. Pulling the skin taut sensitizes the rest of the shaft for your tongue or other hand, while the pressure limits the blood supply.

● The small tube that runs inside the underside of the penis will be extra-sensitive to your tongue—or fingertip.

● If your lover is inclined to have an erection on waking up in the mornings, take it in your mouth. He won't know whether or not he's dreaming!

● Bite and nibble him—let him see your inner animal!

● Play with temperatures—a warm towel and an ice-cube are fun. Alternate the sensation of both, working your way towards his penis.

● Testing it on your own skin first, try dripping candle-wax on his body. Wax is not as painful as it looks, and will awaken his sense of anticipation.

● Now that photography no longer requires sharing your snaps with the drug store, leave a digital camera near your bed, and let him think he thought of playing with it!

foreplay that'll turn her on

It takes women, on average, half an hour from arousal to orgasm. Men, meanwhile, can often come in minutes—so spend the difference making sure your lover is aroused enough to enjoy herself to the fullest, and increase your own pleasure, too. According to surveys, most women want more foreplay, not only for its own sake but also because it is essential for good sex, and sufficient lubrication. These tips show how foreplay moves us smoothly from the cares of life to a sexual space, and a similar care and tenderness can help us come back again.

- The further away from her pleasure points you begin to touch her body, the more fun you'll both have. Spending some time leaving the obvious erogenous zones out of your attentions can paradoxically arouse women more, building tension you'll resolve in due course. She'll love it if it's you teasing her to be patient. Don't forget those "boring" areas like her back and tummy. You don't have to go for the full massage technique—a few gentle strokes will remind her to tune in to her own responses.
- Don't be afraid to use your tongue anywhere—she'll relish sensation in those sensitive spots such as between her toes or the whorl of her anus (but be mindful where you put it afterwards).
- Remember that her skin is probably thinner and more sensitive than yours. A vigor you enjoy may be too much for her, and probably no touch can be too gentle.
- Vary your strokes between lovemaking sessions. Don't get into a routine. Keep her guessing where your next touch will be.
- Nibble at her ear lobes rather than plunging your tongue into her ear. Women tend to enjoy aural touch a bit less than men.
- Tease her breasts—don't reward her expectation of touch straight away. Touch the skin at their edges first. Brush against them as if accidentally, don't forget their often-neglected undersides, and save the nipple for last.
- Before you penetrate her, use the tip of your erect penis to tease her inner thighs and clitoris, making her anticipate what is coming.
- Some women complain that they are touched only when their lover wants sex. Be affectionate to your partner the rest of the time too. Show her that you care for her and are proud to be with her, in private and in public. She may then also be more ready for sex when you are, too!
- Similarly, be thoughtful. A bunch of flowers, a naughty text message, or a sexy surprise in the mail are part of a wider definition of foreplay.
- Finally, it goes without saying, be clean.

watching and pleasuring each other

If you both know how to get the most out of masturbation (see pages 26–31), it could be time to share that with your partner. It's possibly a daunting idea, and one many people are apt to find embarrassing, but if your lover is receptive, it will show them what really turns you on, as they watch precisely where and how you touch yourself. Spend a while being comfortable with each other beforehand—share some wine, if you like, to take the edge off your self-consciousness a little, and show each other a corresponding degree of openness and intimacy. This isn't a flirty strip or a sub-dom game, but a shared show-and-tell of your private sexual pleasures.

Sit down together where you can see each other, with your legs spread. Take a moment to get comfortable. Make sure you have a great, uninterrupted view of your partner's genitalia and what they are about to do with them, but also one in which you will be able to maintain eye-contact throughout: for communication, reassurance, and those sultry looks of pleasure you'll feel like flashing across the room. You will be treated to the sight of your lover's naked body and face as they travel towards their climax.

Have fun turning each other on by drawing attention to the parts of yourself that your lover likes. Have a laugh with each other, but not at each other's expense. If the mood takes you, get a little pornographic: pinch your nipples, making them erect and darker; play with your whole body; pull and pinch your sensitive places; caress yourself; suck your fingers; show yourself to your partner as someone consumed in your own pleasure.

Not only can watching your partner masturbate be an amazing turn-on in itself, but it can seriously benefit your lovemaking, too, by showing you first-hand their most intimate hot-spots and deepest physical turn-ons. Watch closely exactly what it takes to get him or her off. You are being given the privilege of doing something that would otherwise get you arrested, so take the opportunity to learn from it. Notice whether they stop and start or use one continuous movement. Judge how long it takes them. Check what speed they move at and how it increases or decreases at different points—do they speed up when they are closer to climax? Unless they're on the verge of coming, don't be afraid to ask—it makes for horny conversation; or else narrate to each other what you're doing and what turns you on.

See if they touch any parts of themselves that you haven't thought of. When it comes to touching different places, do they have any order of preference? These are the questions worth asking yourself. Perhaps your girlfriend strokes her labia for a long time before moving on to her clitoris. Perhaps your boyfriend cups his balls with one hand until he is closer to orgasm. If either of you is self-conscious, it could help to get physically closer. Reach out and help each other if you like, but don't touch each other's genitals unless you both decide to abandon the exercise in favor of making love. Kiss each other, suck each other's fingers or touch each other's nipples. Play with them, kiss and tease the parts of their body they have been playing with. Not only will you be multiplying sensations you have seen are arousing, you'll reassure your lover that it's OK to carry on pursuing their pleasure.

aftershocks

As much as we put thought into foreplay, we don't always think enough of "afterplay." Often, men and women feel different after he has come. For a period, he will be incapable of responding to stimulation, and will feel a greater or lesser degree of pulling away or even ambivalence towards his partner—this is natural; don't be fazed by it.

Meanwhile, she may not have come, and may still be in the throes of sexual fantasy. At the very least, she will want a cuddle if they decide he won't pleasure her further. While men are inclined to think of sex—for them—as stopping when they come, that doesn't mean it's over yet. After a woman orgasms, she returns to an earlier plateau of sexual arousal rather than the straightforwardly pre-sexual stage to which men revert.

It's up to you both to come down as compatibly as you warmed up. Here are some tips to ensure you both feel happy and satisfied.

- Tell her how much you enjoyed making love.
- If you're inclined to feel moody after coming, finish on top, where you can simply hold her quietly.
- Keep tissues and water on hand. Having to rush off and clean up breaks the spell. Offer to wipe her, too.
- Unless you're both getting off on fantasies of anonymity or being used, a cuddle or affirmation of pleasure is especially important after furtive, quickie sex.

sex with someone you love

Not only is masturbation a marvelous way to spend some time, it is also the best way of exploring your own body and sexual fantasies. As in the real thing, we can all use a little foreplay. It's important not to feel inhibited with yourself. It's the exception when people of either sex reach orgasm by physical sensations alone, and it's utterly okay to have any sexual fantasy you like: they're just that—fantasies.

for her

Make your foreplay-for-one physical as well as psychological. Trace your fingers over your body before you touch yourself intimately; pinch your nipples; bite your lips. The more you anticipate touching your genitals, the more alive they will feel.

- Don't be ashamed to accessorize: if you're given to fantasizing directly about your lover, perhaps a piece of clothing that they have worn recently might be at hand. Otherwise, take a look around your closet or home—is there any object with a safe, secondary use as self-bondage toy or sex aid (see pages 108–115)? Don't be embarrassed—you'll be using exactly the same inventiveness that made us a dominant species!

- Speaking of evolution, there's a small design flaw in the human female: when you're on your back, your vaginal juices need a little help getting up to your clitoris. There's no harm in helping things along with a little water-based lubricant. Nevertheless, some degree of friction is necessary to reach orgasm, so if you're too slippery, you'll know that you've used too much.

- Many women's first orgasm happens in a shower. Held against the clitoris for a moment or two, a shower head can have you holding on for balance. Some like hot tubs for the same reason. Having said that, too direct an aim at the vagina can tear delicate skin there and disturb your pH balance. It could also desensitize you too quickly to pursue your pleasure. Try teasing yourself with a gentle but inexorable trickle of water over the clitoris.

- Vibrators and dildos are out of the closet. They are no longer marketed solely as massage aids, and quite a few cities have at least one specialist female-friendly sex-aid store. If you normally concentrate on your clitoris when you masturbate, try it with the sensation of being filled with a dildo, as your vaginal muscles will contract furiously during orgasm in any case.

- Despite its shape, a vibrator comes into its own on the clitoris. Start with a slow setting, just hold it there, and find out what works for you. For a hands-free experience, squeeze your knees together to clamp a vibrator at the top of your thighs. Many people dislike the noise of a vibe. As a rule, you get what you pay for: rubber-sheathed ones tend to sound more muted than hard plastic, and a condom, apart from providing essential hygiene, can insulate noise a little further.

- Some vibrators can be exceptionally vigorous. Take care to always start with a low setting and build up to what you can bear, in order not to bruise delicate tissue.

get comfy

Lying or sitting back with your legs spread is the most popular way for women to masturbate. Naked is good but, equally—depending on how sensitive you are—don't forget the delicious effects of the different materials and fabrics from which underwear is made. Pressing the soles of your feet together will increase the tension in your groin. As you stroke, circle or flick your clitoris, tease yourself by stopping and starting your steady rhythm, staving off your climax as long as you can bear. Most people increase their stimulation before they come, and you will most likely have found what is right for you.

You can lie with your buttocks upwards, face-down on the bed. Rub against something—vibrator, pillow, or hairbrush—or anything that arouses your interest. Your whole body can move up and down against the bed, providing stimulation for sensitive spots like your stomach and pubic area—the parts of the body that are usually used to skin-on-skin contact during lovemaking. It also allows you to buck and move your hips as you would during the real thing, which can be an additional, powerful incentive to reach orgasm. For a change, try reaching around to arouse yourself from behind, and see how that feels.

for him

Many men learned to masturbate in snatched moments of privacy away from a parent or guardian. You're a grown-up now, with your own space, so take a few moments to relax and center yourself.

- You may be more or less used to using a lubricant. Try a water-based lube—they will mimic best the velvety smoothness of a vagina.
- Alternated with your strokes, try holding your cock at its base and stroking with your fingertips from the head to the base. Tease yourself—you're in control.
- Don't be mean—condoms aren't just for intercourse. You'll save on tissues and spare yourself the bother of cleaning up afterwards, especially if you're planning to drift off to sleep.
- Imagine it's someone else's hands giving you pleasure. A pair of gloves will help. Roughness and seams can hurt, though, and you may not want to get them messy with lube. As smooth as possible is best—and kinkiest!
- Let your body feel as free to move and buck around as it would during the real thing. Don't be self-conscious: make some noise.
- Break a rut. If you've become used to masturbating with a certain lazy ritual, change your plans. If you use pornography, try fantasy alone, or vice versa. Try different rooms and positions.

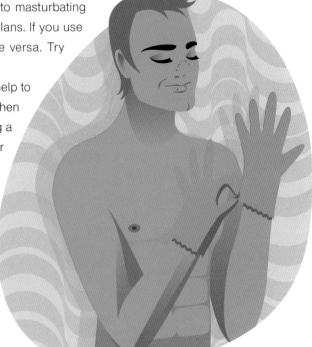

- The warm steam of a bathroom will help to get your blood flowing where it counts. When you're in the bath or shower, try directing a shower jet upwards at your perineum, for external stimulation of the prostate.
- Don't hurry to clean yourself up. Have a towel or tissues at hand, so you don't have to move right away. Feel your breathing slow up and your body relax.

the twin functions of male masturbation

Most men, most of the time, want to masturbate to a tension-relieving orgasm by the shortest route, and there is nothing wrong with that goal-centered approach! But delaying your own orgasm once in a while can teach you ways that will make you more confident during the real thing, to the pleasure of you and your partner. It would be especially useful to research the methods mentioned here further if you find you come before you'd like to from time to time.

When you feel you are about to come, simply stop fantasizing for a while. But don't let worries intrude—the aim is also to maintain your erection. You don't have to be an expert in Tantra to think about how you are breathing and to try to pace your breaths evenly. Slowing your heart rate will delay that point of no return and a little breath-control goes a long way to heading off the moment when you can't hold back. It will make for a more satisfying orgasm in the end and, carried over into your lovemaking, may make for a more satisfied partner.

As your body prepares to come, your testicles contract against the base of your penis. Cupping all of their surface areas to avoid twisting them, pull your balls gently away from your cock. This is one to try when you have a little time before your orgasm, as it requires gradual movement, a little care, and it doesn't work as fast as pushing a button. If you are closer to orgasm, try pressing down—or up—on your perineum with your fingertips. If you are standing, you will find you can reach it from behind. If you're sitting or lying down, then front is best. Not only does this interrupt the readiness of the urethra to force your semen along it, it makes for a curiously pleasant feeling—different to orgasm—in itself. Having a trusted partner perform these last two for you, especially during penetration, can benefit your lovemaking greatly.

going down

Women and men alike, in all sorts of sexology surveys, from magazines to academic studies, report wanting more oral sex in their relationships. This section tells you how to master the art of oral, from a basic blow job to tip-tingling tricks of the trade; and from accomplished cunnilingus to advanced oral teases for adventurous lovers!

going down a treat

Whatever it's called—cunnilingus, licking her out, going down on her—it is practically bound to give her an orgasm when it's done well.

Women love oral sex because it's soft, wet, and friction-free, and doesn't leave them feeling sore. So there's no need to wear out your tongue by using it as a mini-penis, thrusting it in and out of the vagina. The best results come from concentrating on the clitoris. Kiss her labia the same way that you might kiss the lips on her face. Circle around the clitoris; don't make a beeline straight for it. Try not to stretch her too wide at any time in order to see what you are doing. Smother, cover, and lick her with the surface of your tongue rather than flicking at her clitoris with its tip right away.

As they become engorged during arousal, some clitorises resemble a tiny penis. Feel how the hood (prepuce) can move back and forth over the clitoral bud in a similar way to the movement of a foreskin.

Being careful not to pull too sharply, create a more taut, accessible surface for your tongue, and expose more sensitive skin by holding the top of her labia open with one hand, making the clitoris easier to find. Or ask her to do it, so that your hands are free to caress the rest of her body.

Use your hands, too. Caress her breasts, run your fingers through her pubic hair, stroke and massage her clitoral lips, buttocks, and inner thighs. With your palm upwards, slip a finger or two inside her. Doing it gradually is the key, taking care not to surprise or stretch her vagina before it is fully relaxed to your touch. Your fingernails, of course, should be short. If your fingers are inside your partner to the knuckle, then with a steady, gentle, massaging motion, draw the pads of your fingers across the roof of her vagina. Apply a gentle pressure, not being afraid to leave them still from time to time as you focus with your tongue on her clitoris.

You will feel a patch of undulating skin beyond the mouth of the vagina, which is rougher to the touch, not unlike the roof of your mouth. This is the location of the much-debated G-spot (see page 14), so pay particular attention to your lover's reactions as your fingers apply pressure here.

It is vital to maintain a slow, steady rhythm, letting her get used to what you're doing. If she's showing that she's enjoying what you're doing, that means keep on exactly at that pace: don't step it up.

Use the top and bottom of your tongue. Rough and smooth, they produce very different sensations. If you lick at her vagina, you will notice that your nose nuzzles

naturally into the top of her vulva. Burying your face into her like this while your tongue is thrusting inside will give her vaginal and clitoral stimulation. Be patient, orgasm can take awhile, especially if this is the first part of foreplay. Your partner will become especially self-conscious if you betray impatience, and will be much less likely to come at all. Better still, show your enthusiasm. Immerse yourself in your partner's natural tastes and smells and give yourself extra time to get even more aroused.

m' lady's pleasure

In the most well-known cunnilingus position, your partner lies back on the edge of a bed or chair with your head between her parted legs. All she has to do is lie back and enjoy—but if she likes, she can spread and tighten her legs and move her hips to guide you. Remember that our bodies are unique, individual, and always differ from any diagram. The chances are that she'll be more sensitive on one side of her clitoris. If her legs are spread wide enough, you can explore until your tongue finds her most sensitive area. Place one of her legs over your shoulder and you'll find you can bury your face in her further, penetrating her more easily with your tongue. She can move her hips more easily in time with your motion, too.

get hip

Instead of crouching or lying between her opened legs, try kneeling at the edge of the bed or couch she's lying on, with both of her legs over your shoulders. Supporting part of her weight, you will hold her almost upside-down. If you lock your arms around her hips, you are in control. Your view will be a real turn-on. At this angle, too, you can really bury your tongue into her vagina or tease her clitoris with it, along with your mouth and nose. As if the excitement weren't enough, the blood will rush to her head, too!

lean on me

Ask a lover to sit on your face. You may need to hold your breath from time to time if her buttocks and thighs smother you, but once you're in a regular rhythm you'll find yourself moving naturally to draw breath without interrupting her arousal.

The beauty of this position is that you will truly find out from her precisely where she gets turned on. Lie still while she moves her vagina and clitoris over your mouth, tongue and nose and, when you're confident of what she likes, move your tongue against her. If it helps, bring your face closer to her, and to prevent your neck from aching, make sure your head is on a pillow.

Move your tongue up and down and alternate this with sucking firmly, until you reach a rhythm that you can't let go of! If she faces your feet, you can tease her anus and her perineum, although facing the other way is best for clitoral stimulation.

Although this position feels great, she may find it a bit of a strain, and may have to maintain a constant effort with her thigh muscles not to crush you. It may be more comfortable for her to lean forward.

knee-trembler

For a quick thrill, try doing it with her standing up and with her legs parted. This can be very sexy if she's wearing a skirt without pantyhose. Kneel in front of her and brush your tongue upwards against her clitoris. You can wrap your arms around the backs of her thighs and feel her vagina with your fingers as your tongue goes to work, or push her towards you to make her pubic mound more pronounced.

heaven scents

The French have a word for the female genital smell—*la cassolette*, or the little perfume box. Some women say they're unable to enjoy oral sex because they are concerned about their personal hygiene; they worry that their partners will be turned off if their vaginas don't have a chemically enhanced freshness at all times. However, the natural musky smell you give off is packed with pheromones and is a powerful aphrodisiac. Showering once or twice a day and using a conventional soap should keep you as fresh as you need to be. Constantly freshening yourself with douches and scented products could actually damage the delicate pH balance of your vagina and do more harm than good. If you're genuinely worried about a bad smell coming from there, have a word with your doctor, as it could be a sign of an infection.

True to form, a lot of pleasurable things can affect the way you smell and taste: alcohol, coffee, and cigarettes, for example. At the other end of the scale, a light vegetarian diet will keep you as sweet as possible. There's also the question of pubic hair. Some men love natural bushiness while others go wild at the sight of a bare pair of labial lips. Cropping your hairs will, for you, result in greater sensitivity.

fabulous fellatio

"Blow job" is, of course, a horribly inaccurate term. It's all about sucking. Some men crave lots of sucking, while others prefer being taken in your mouth as something to be traded off with tricks and licks along the way. Running your fingers softly through his pubic hair before you begin will not only wake up his skin arousingly but will free any loose pubic hairs beforehand that might otherwise get stuck in your teeth.

Like you, he may take time to get aroused, so don't grab hold of him and masturbate furiously from the start. Fellate him softly until he becomes fully hard, and don't feel insecure if he isn't immediately standing at attention—he may be feeling that it is required of him, too.

Draw your lips over your teeth into an "O" shape before going anywhere near his erect penis. (Snagging the head of his cock with your teeth is guaranteed to have him waiting in fear for it to happen again!) Make full use of your tongue. Relaxed, wide and spread, it is perfect for stroking and caressing every inch of him as you run it up his shaft. Clenched and firm, it's a strong muscle capable of providing extremely intense stimulation once you're underway.

Pay attention to the extra-sensitive areas of his penis, such as the large vein that runs beneath it and the rim around its head. His glans—located at the point where the urethra underneath meets the hood—really is sensitive, so take care not to exert unbearable pressure there. Fast, light, flicking licks will help to wake up the surface of his penis, and give renewed stiffness to a flagging erection.

Don't forget his testicles! Although switching attention may diminish his erection a little, this doesn't mean it's turning him off—more that his whole genital area is becoming erogenized! During the later stages of arousal, when his testes have contracted, pulling them gently downwards against his shaft is a technique for delaying orgasm. However, his balls are very sensitive to unusual twists and turns, especially when it comes to fellatio, so take care to concentrate on their skin.

Drawing either surface of your tongue across the sensitive skin of his scrotal sac will have him basking in pleasure; your tongue will tug at his pubic hairs and make them tingle. This technique will delight him if you use it on his testicles, because the tiny hairs on his balls can be pulled and snagged by the surface of the top of your tongue. Try alternating this with series of light flicks. The line that runs along the center of his scrotal sac is especially sensitive, too. For an extra good vibration, try humming as you take one of his balls gently between your lips.

Unless it is part of a wider game, don't just let him move your head to his chosen rhythm; this is about you taking control. You can master his thrusts and increase his pleasure, by making a ring with your thumb and fingers at the base of his penis. Not only does this put a brake on his thrusts, leaving your mouth and tongue freer to do their work, your fingers will mimic a cock-ring, maintaining his erection, creating an extension of your lips, and making penetration feel deep to the hilt.

If your throat can take it, he will love going deep into your mouth, where the shape formed by the surface of your tongue, slightly rough on his sensitive underside, together with your soft palette, form the perfect shape to stimulate the head of his penis. If you have a sensitive gag reflex, then don't feel pressured into taking him that deep, but a little practice (even with an inanimate object) may help to overcome it. In addition to making a ring around the base of his penis, you might like to try using your hands to play with his balls as you suck him. Press down on his perineum when he's about to come though, and his pleasure will be increased immeasurably.

If your mouth is getting a little tired, you can move his penis from the middle of your mouth to your cheek. Remember, it will increase his pleasure if you withdraw his penis completely from your mouth every so often, close your lips once more around its head then take him in your mouth afresh. Every time, he'll be treated to the arousing sight of his penis entering you, while closing your lips around the head of his penis and sliding down mimics the feeling of entering a vagina. You can take the opportunity to pay attention each time to the extra-sensitive tip of his penis with your tongue.

the courtesan

He lies or kneels over you on his hands and knees and places his penis in your mouth. Your fingers in a ring around the base of his penis will prevent him pushing too far. You will, however, need to be relaxed to accommodate his penis. Propping your head on a pillow will help you reach him.

the domestic help

Kneeling at his feet is the classic blow-job position of male fantasy. Have him standing—great for the shower! He will feel that you are being completely subservient to his desires, and that he is all-powerful. But, as you look up and catch his eye seductively, you will know that you are in control. Your knees may get a little sore so you might like to have a cushion handy.

the temptress

The most popular position, though, is for him to lie back on a bed or couch, his legs parted enough for you to kneel between them. In this position, you can reach around to cup and knead his buttocks, or up to pinch his nipples. It requires a bit of work, but you'll look so slinky as you're doing it, and he will feel utterly pampered and grateful.

spit or swallow?

You should not feel under any pressure either way. Once he's past that point of no return, your man shouldn't really mind what you do with a mouthful of his come. And I'll let you in on a locker-room secret—he probably doesn't mind. Even if it's part of his fantasy that you swallow, it won't seem so important once the time arrives—he'll be too busy basking gratefully in post-coital pleasure.

If you and your man want to be low-down and dirty, let him come on your face and breasts (taking care to avoid your eyes—ejaculate stings). For many men this is an incredibly arousing sight—not for nothing is it a staple ingredient of pornography—and it may mean more to him than the abstract fact of whether or not you swallow his come. Whatever you do, do what you are comfortable with, since acting revolted seconds after he's ejaculated will ruin your good intentions anyway.

If you are both partial to his being sucked deeply until he ejaculates, then you're likely to discover its an acquired taste. Keep a glass of something beside you to refresh your mouth, together with tissues into which you can spit discreetly. Eating the right diet can improve the taste of semen—fruit will sweeten it, while spicy foods, alcohol, coffee, red meat, and tobacco make it more sour.

It should be clear when he's about to come from his increasing enthusiasm and his moans of pleasure. But if you're nervous of being taken by surprise, ask him to let you know with a quick word or a gentle signal such as a tug of your hair.

course of pleasure

If you are both practiced at the basic techniques of fellatio and cunnilingus, you might want to experiment with other styles of oral sex that will appeal to your sense of adventure.

deep throat

He kneels at the edge of the bed or sofa, and you lie back with your head hanging down off the edge of the bed and your mouth open. The aim is to create as long a passage as possible for his penis. Ask him to be gentle with his thrusts—not everyone can pull this off and your throat needs to be very relaxed. If you feel choked, switch to a more comfortable position.

rimming

More correctly known as anilingus, rimming is the delicate act of using your tongue to stimulate your lover's anus, and can be enjoyed by men and women alike. Lick around the anus with your tongue, using your hands to pull the buttocks slightly apart. Move your tongue in circular, flicking movements around the thin skin there, or, clenching your tongue muscle, poke firmly into it. Be cautious with hygiene though, and do not return to pleasuring your partner's penis or vulva without rinsing first. The recipient should be fresh from the tub, and the giver should not have any sores or cuts on the soft skin around their mouth, which is particularly susceptible to infection. When done well though, rimming can bring your partner a whole different set of teasing, relaxing sensations.

sixty-nine

No prizes for guessing how this got its name. Go head to toe, so that you can give each other oral sex simultaneously. It's not as easy as it sounds to give and receive pleasure at the same time, so don't feel pressured to have a great time the first time. Focusing on your own sensations may distract you from giving pleasure to your lover, but sometimes they feel so good that it can't be helped. The very idea of simultaneous oral sex is a great turn-on in itself, so persevere if the earth doesn't move for both of you right away.

Sixty-nine is perfect for those times when coming isn't the immediate goal, or when you're both so horny that the merest messing-around will bring you to orgasm.

Being exactly the same height is not, of course, high up on the list of things we look for in a potential partner, so different couples will have varying degrees of success at Sixty-nine. But the beauty of it is that it really feels that you are trading off equal pleasure with each other, and you may find that you slip naturally into the way of taking turns that suits you best. Spending time switching the attention between one another's genitals can build up to a big orgasm for both of you.

You may mutually find that this is the easiest position, for the simple reason that women tend to be lighter than men. He lies on his back, with his arms beside him or cupping her buttocks. She crouches on all fours with her bottom in the air, over his face, and rests on her forearms. Her mouth is ready, directly above his penis. She can control the rhythm of the head she's receiving by moving her hips back and forth in time, and she's perfectly positioned to pay attention to every inch of his shaft. If she arches her back, she can brush her breasts against his stomach, turning him on and stimulating her own nipples too. His arms are free to caress her. His fingers can reach inside her vagina, while her fingers are free enough to encircle the base of his shaft.

If he crouches over her on all fours, he will enjoy the control he has in pleasuring her, with lots of room to find what turns her on. He is in a perfect position to play with her breasts or part her labia, and can see exactly what he's doing. His neck won't ache from having to raise his head, which he can rest on her inner thighs, as he watches his fingers or explores with his tongue. It is not easy for her to take him fully between her lips, but she can masturbate him perfectly, holding the base of his penis and teasing its tip, or arouse him further by drawing his cock around her cheeks, neck, and breasts.

glad all over

Physical touch is necessary for our well-being. When people don't get enough touch as babies and children, their emotional growth is stunted. Touch is a practical symbol of love and care that we all need. A simple hug has the power to cure our blues!

A loving massage of our whole body leaves us feeling relaxed, cared for, and rejuvenated. If you've yet to focus on massage with a partner, there's no better time than now. Massage is a style of sensual touch that can be sexual or non-sexual. Everyone loves a good massage, so it's a good way of building physical trust between you, and a good opportunity to get to know each other's bodies in a safe, intimate way.

preparation

confidence

According to holistic theories of medicine, the power of touch can be one of the most genuine healers and stress relievers in the world. Sometimes lovers don't give a good massage because they are lazy, but sometimes, too, it's because they are a little shy. Like dancing, if you don't think you're any good, then you are less likely to give yourself the chance to improve. No one likes to be a loser. But massage is essentially about loving touch, which is central to being a lover.

If you are not sure what makes for a proper massage, the quickest way to find out is to treat yourself to one! Your local gym or community center will be able to help you find a qualified practitioner. It's worth the money—experiencing the benefits for yourself will give you a personal understanding of what to aim for that you won't find in books. This way you will know how different strokes will feel to your lover. In the meantime, however, this section will give you some essentials that will show you that you don't have to spend a year in an Indian ashram before you can give a good massage.

intimate favors

Holistic medicine emphasizes the close relationship between your body and your mind. When we are troubled, our bodies tense, and tension in the body can exacerbate mental stress, too. A sensual massage is about relaxing and relieving stress and tension in the body, interrupting the cycle. It will help your lover's mind, lessening the impact of their cares and woes. In time, you will automatically come to know where a regular partner holds their tension.

Make your massage a gift: put your lover at their ease. Explain to them that you're doing this because you want to and not because you expect one in return. Give it for the sake of giving. Only then will they be able to focus on themselves and become completely relaxed. If they want to return the favor, they can do so another day.

Although a massage is about health and wellness, it can be erotic, arousing, and exciting as well as healing. It is unusual to the Western mind, to mention arousal and healing in the same breath. But to the Eastern philosophies on which massage techniques are based, it is the whole being that is important, and that includes our sexual centers, too. This does not mean that erotic massage has to end in sexual play, but it might lead to a heightened state of sexual pleasure.

Although massage techniques can be part of foreplay, however, it is vital never to begin a massage with the assumption that it will end in intercourse. Asking your lover for sex or trying to "get them going" will undo all your good work, resulting in your partner feeling stressed and begrudging their favor.

Erotic massage can include the genitals and erogenous zones, but it doesn't have to. If it does, your partner must feel completely free to focus on the sensations you are causing, and not on what signals you are trying to give. Giving them cause to wonder will create a source of tension. Follow through on your promise, and have no intentions beyond giving them peace and pleasure.

Through your touch and your lover's feedback, you will discover which techniques they like, where they hold tension in their body, how much pressure is ideal, and what parts need a little extra T.L.C. In a more extended massage, you will help them to get to know their own bodies more deeply, too: it's not uncommon to hear the phrase, "I didn't know I had a muscle there." As they become more intimate with themselves, almost incidentally, you will open pathways that will later make for deeper sexual communication.

a sense of ritual

It is important to signal that you're giving a massage, so your partner feels completely free to relax, as much as they would if they were paying for the privilege. Make sure the environment is warm and cosy. Your lover's body temperature will drop as they will not be moving around, and the cold can, in turn, make a body tense up. Soft lighting is similarly essential as—although most of the time we don't notice—bright light makes us tense, too.

The person being massaged should lie on a firm surface—a decent mattress or a futon is ideal. A carpeted floor is also suitable—and much better than a saggy old mattress—but it should be clean and covered with a sheet or towels. Keep additional towels around to cover the areas you have just attended to, so they stay warm, as well as to catch drips from massage oils. Depending upon taste, unsyncopated, ambient music is known to slow our breathing and heart rates.

Make sure you have as much space as possible around you. Your lover should feel free to stretch their limbs to the fullest, and you will need a wider area to move around in than your lover does to lie in, so don't forget to factor that in, too. Smell is crucial, as your partner will be breathing deeply, so if you don't have a taste for burning essential oils or incense, at least make sure your space is freshly aired (though warm) and free from cooking or tobacco smells. You will be exerting yourself, so don't forget a glass of liquid for yourself along with the massage oil. You don't want to have to interrupt proceedings by dashing to the kitchen. On a similar note, check that neither of you needs the bathroom, and switch off your phones.

Take off your finger rings. Before you start the massage, first pay a moment's attention to how you feel. Take some deep breaths, feel your feet connected to the floor, and let mental distractions go. Like good sex, giving a great massage requires your full presence. Find the peace and strength in yourself that you would like to give to your partner.

oils

Although you can give and get a perfectly good back rub without oils, it is essential for applying rigorous pressure to those deep-down knotted muscles without causing friction burns on the skin. And the hairier your partner, the more oil you will need. You can use baby oil or body lotion, but the best is a purpose-made massage oil, preferably neutral, such as peachnut or almond. There's a vast range of essential oils available, too, along with several premixed scented oils. Be aware, though, that most neat essential oils are far too powerful to apply undiluted to the skin.

Don't make your lover jump with a splash of cold oil. Popping its container into a mug of warm water for a while beforehand will do the trick, but it's just as well to warm it vigorously between your hands, which will warm them too, of course.

the massage

The first touch should be a simple laying of hands on your lover's body. Begin with their lower back, move up their spine, applying a little more pressure as you go, telling them to breathe and release. These moments are about connecting, not giving them a shock. Aim to work on one area at a time, and then move to others. You might start with their shoulders, arms, and neck, work down their back and hips, and on to their buttocks, thighs, and calves.

Don't forget their hands and feet. These bear so much of life's physical stresses and have much to benefit from being loosened, manipulated, and gently massaged. Talking is best kept to a minimum. If you are planning to relax knotted muscles, build gradually to the required firmness. Your partner will tense if you shock them with vigor or pressure right away. When your lover is on their front, raise and turn their head gently on the flat surface from time to time. When necessary, help to turn them onto their back, cradling their head and causing them to use as few of their own muscles as possible. As you proceed, you will learn to listen for the little clicks and pops that denote areas of tension, and to feel and return to the knots within your partner's muscles.

techniques

long strokes

These are designed to run the length of your lover's body, either from their buttocks to the tips of their shoulders, or from the ankle to the buttocks. If your partner is on their back, you can use these strokes from their shoulders, across their chest and down to the bottom of their abdomen, too. No serious pressure should be applied to joints, so use light touches around wrists, elbows, ankles, and knees.

Most of us instinctively use the flat of our hands when rubbing someone, and this is perfect for beginning your attentions on a fresh area. Apply pressure when stroking away from your body, and a lighter, brushing motion on the return. This way the flat of your palm will do most of the work. Move up your lover's body, to contrast with the usual feeling of gravity, relaxing muscles and preparing them for deeper strokes. Sit astride your lover and move your hands upwards from their hips, towards their shoulders, and returning more lightly down the outside. Cupping your hands and using their outer edges is ideal for applying a little pressure on the downward stroke, to loosen muscle fiber, if you so choose.

These long strokes are perfect for warming the muscles prior to deeper work or, at the end, to calm them down again. Keep on moving, and don't break contact with your partner's body all of a sudden. If possible, trail your fingers along their skin to the next part to be massaged.

Cupping your hands, but using your whole palm, is great for the thighs and calf muscles, where many people carry tension. Sitting astride your lover, but facing their feet, is best for this. Start just above the ankles, with your hands next to each other, and draw them towards you, exerting less pressure on the return. It is easy to alternate this with squeezing motions, or to concentrate with both hands on one calf or thigh muscle, stretching it between them with enough pressure to help flush waste matter through the bloodstream to the lymph glands.

In the Swiss school of massage, these long strokes are known as *effleurage*. Used vigorously, they will stimulate and invigorate, while medium strokes will relax, and lighter strokes tickle the epidermis, focusing your lover's attention on your chosen area.

squeezing

Wringing and squeezing motions will help to release tension and relax the muscles, and the ones that lend themselves best to these techniques are the legs, buttocks, and shoulders. Squeezing helps to break up the knots caused by emotional turmoil, stress, repetitious working patterns, and other imbalances that impact on our bodies and will continue to cause us discomfort if they are not kneaded out.

Use your thumbs as well as your fingers, and think of kneading dough, squeezing and rolling pliable areas of flesh between them. Use your body weight to lean into your movements as much as you think your partner can bear, and be sure to feel for knots and kinks as you go. Known as *petrissage*, this technique can break down fatty tissues and get the blood flowing again. Slow, deep squeezes will help to release tension and toxins (in our modern world of office work, this is especially good for the shoulders) while faster kneading will increase stimulation, energizing the body. You can knead an entire muscle area with a fluid motion or focus on a particular spot.

Here are some typical tricks that involve long strokes or squeezing.

• With your hands an inch or two apart, wring your partner's arm or leg as if you are wringing out a towel, moving up and down the length of the limb. This alternates well with plucking and shaking the muscle. Be sure to have a sense of how much pressure they're comfortable with, checking verbally, if necessary.

• While kneeling to one side of them, lay both hands, thumbs together, on a buttock or thigh. Move firmly across the muscle with the heels of your palms. You can work your way down the leg like this, but be sure to do both buttocks or legs for balance.

• A treat for the arms or legs: place your hands together at your wrists, just beneath the joint of the limb that you wish to move away from. Lining up your fingers so that they point towards hand or foot, cup as much muscle as you can into your palms. Push and knead it vigorously from side to side, move a hand's length down and repeat until you've moved down the limb.

• Anchor your lover's limb at the ankle or wrist with one hand as you cup, stroke, and squeeze towards their body with the other. This will give you something to pull away from, and balance the naturally anchoring effect of their body weight. Be sure to hold the limb as firmly outstretched as is comfortable, to deep-stretch the muscles.

all fingers and thumbs

Use the pads of your thumbs to apply pressure to particular points on your lover's body, either because they are hard to get to, or because you're hunting down an individual knot that you detected while stroking. You can use both thumbs together, holding your hands still against your partner for balance if the added pressure of your body weight is required. Or you can dig with the thumbs themselves into those out-of-the-way places, such as under the shoulder blades, between the ribs to either side of (but at least ½ in. away from) the spine, or at the tie-in points of the muscles in their limbs.

If your thumbs are tired, you can use your knuckles, too. Rock them back and forth in a line against a stubborn knot or where you want to apply pressure, especially on the back or chest. For more fleshy areas, use plenty of oil, make a full fist, and draw your knuckles smoothly down in a gliding motion.

percussive maintenance

Percussive movements are good for breaking up fatty and toxic deposits and generally waking an area up. Take care to stay away from injured or especially bony areas. It is safe for the larger areas of muscle tissue such as the buttocks and thighs, and especially for the trapezius, the muscle that sits across the top of your shoulders like a yoke, where many people hold a lot of tension. Keep your wrists loose and your hands relaxed, and maintain a steady rhythm with no surprises.

• To gently prepare an area for deeper massage, try tapping lightly with your fingertips. It feels fantastic when alternated with stroking. This is also great for sensitive areas such as the face, bony places, and the scalp.

• Open your hand and try a regular, relaxed, rhythmic, karate-style chop with the underside. This is worth trying after a period of strokes, following their direction of travel across the shoulders, buttocks, or legs, efficiently relaxing surface muscles for deeper attention to the ones beneath them.

• You can close your hand loosely into a fist and pound downwards on larger, more fleshy areas, being careful to use the softer flesh on your wrists, the heels of your palms, and your fingers. This works well when alternated with some deep squeezing.

other techniques

- Tugging, pulling, and pinching the skin between thumb and forefinger will break up the tension across an area; done lightly but firmly, it will bring the blood flowing to the surface of the skin. Or else try pinching a calf, arm, back, or shoulder muscle, raising it gently away from the bone and wobbling it to shake out the tension before a kneading stroke.

- Try placing your forearm diagonally across your partner's back and, being careful to avoid the spine, put your body weight behind it and move it in a deep swathe to push the shoulder blade outwards and upwards. Rubbing your forearm up and down carefully but deeply between the shoulder blades, parallel with but some distance from the spine, will loosen those deep back muscles. Whatever you do, complete the parallel action on the other side.

- Use your fingers and thumbs to work deep into an area, with a tight, circular motion.

- Sometimes it can be powerfully relaxing to slow gently to a stop, leaving your hands still against your lover's body, breathing deeply, and letting the warmth pass between you.

- Long, feather-light strokes make a great finisher. Run your fingertips lightly down your lover's entire body, extending all the way to the ends of their fingers and toes. Include their scalp, temples, and face, stroke from the hands to the feet on each side, and back again. Lighten the pressure of the strokes until your massage ends imperceptibly.

genital massage

Massage doesn't have to lead to sex, but this doesn't mean that your lover's genitals don't need a massage, too. Many massages bypass breasts, buttocks, and genitals because those areas are sexual; but they are tissue, too, and need massage and therapeutic touch as much as any other part of the body. How often do they get a massage for its own sake, instead of with the goal of sexual excitement?

Relaxing the genitals can make them flower or respond, as you release the tension carried there. If you both have the energy when you are finished, it could be the best warm-up to lovemaking; if either of you isn't in the mood, just cuddle up.

for her

Make sure your hands are thoroughly clean. With your lover on her back, kneel between her legs and gently part them, letting them stay flat. Before beginning a vaginal massage, spend some time working around the abdomen and inner thighs and a few seconds gently cupping her vulva. Gently pinch and roll the sensitive inner and outer labia between your thumbs and forefingers. Work your way slowly up and down each lip simultaneously.

Run your thumbs gently along each side of the clitoral shaft, and all the way down the inner lips. Rub gently with a thumb just inside the area enclosed by the inner labia (the vestibule) taking care not to irritate her urethra opening. For an astonishingly intimate experience, circle gently with both thumb tips until every inch of the labia is massaged. Slip an index finger just barely inside her vaginal opening, and apply a small, circular motion around the inner edges, as if you were feeling the fit of a shirt collar. Work your way around the inside like a clock, stopping at each hour, one through twelve, to continue the circular motion. Be gentle, and cup her vulva for a minute or so once you have finished. Be aware of the tensions women hold there, and the feelings that can be released.

for him

Men are sometimes sensitive about the size of their penis when it is flaccid, so this, too, is definitely one for partners you're comfortable with. With your man on his back, take his penis gently in one hand and rest it on his stomach. Taking care not to pull his hairs too much, pinch the skin of his scrotum gently between thumb and forefinger, to wake it up. You can pull gently on his testicles, being careful not to twist them, but most deserving of your attention is the hidden store of tension beneath his perineum. Using the pad of your thumbs, feel the point where his penis really begins, down there underneath his balls. Apply gentle, circular pressure here, and move both thumbs upwards together in parallel, stopping every ½ in. to continue your circular motion. On the way, push very gently inwards beneath the scrotum, releasing tension in the hidden part of his shaft and reminding him how big his penis really is! Rub your thumbs together briefly around the base of his penis just above the scrotum, and return to his perineum along his inner thigh.

the raunchiest positions

Even the most legendary lovers from history, male or female, will most likely have fallen into a routine from time to time. We all have our favorite routine, and, at times when simply finding the time to make love is an achievement in itself, there's no shame in easing into comfortable positions we know we'll enjoy. However, it's worth remembering that, when it comes to sexual pleasure, even just a little variation can introduce a whole lot of new sensations.

he's on top

the missionary position

This is the most common sexual position, of course, and the one most of us think of first. Its reputation for being boring, however, is undeserved. Just because it's the most natural position, that doesn't mean it has to be lazy sex.

Missionary sex is powerfully erotic: top-to-toe skin contact, which enlivens and awakens the body, is greater than in any other position. The man is able to exercise his full physical power, thrusting his hips at their most natural angle of approach. There is very little effort involved for the woman, who is at her most open and passive. Eye-contact, kissing, and talking are possible throughout. Other parts of her body are readily accessible, whether it's nibbling her ears or caressing her breasts that most excites her.

She lies on her back with her legs parted; he lies over her, supporting his weight on his elbows and thrusts once he is inside her. It's part of the fun if it takes a guiding hand. Missionary sex offers little for the woman who wants to take the lead, and it's not renowned for offering great clitoral stimulation. However, there are ways of maintaining her clitoral arousal despite the fact that missionary sex offers most of its sensation vaginally.

Placing a pillow or cushion underneath her hips alters the tilt of her pelvis, opening her clitoris to much more friction against his pelvic bone than when she is flat on the bed. If you are both enjoying a slower pace of intimate missionary sex, then an alternative to the man burying himself to the hilt in his partner involves him withdrawing slightly as he continues to thrust, supporting his own weight, and slipping a hand, palm downwards, gently down her stomach until his fingertips find her clitoris.

legs inside

This variation on the missionary will spice it up: she lies on her back and spreads her legs so that he can penetrate her. Once he's inside, however, instead of wrapping her legs around the outside of his, she slides them down so that they're straight, running inside his legs, like closed scissors.

This position can lengthen her vagina, making for a new range of penetrative feelings (and accommodating him better if he's extra-well endowed); squeezing her legs together will stimulate her clitoris, and she can squeeze against his penis with her vaginal muscle more strongly than when they're apart.

Using her hands, she can push his buttocks until he is deeper inside her. Otherwise, she has less control than in many positions, which makes this position fun if she enjoys a feeling of helplessness. With her arms by her sides, it's ideal for a bit of light-hearted bondage (see pages 104–107).

I surrender

From a kneeling position, she leans backwards until she is lying on the bed with her legs folded beneath her. She may raise her arms above her head as he lies on top of her. Her breasts are stretched taught, sensitive to his touch and the skin of his chest, and meanwhile other parts of her body, such as her sides, are more accessible than usual to his touch.

the "flower press"

She lies back and he kneels on the bed in front of her with his legs parted. She brings her knees right up to her chin, so that her feet are on his chest, or over his shoulders and either side of his head. With his knees on the bed, either side of her buttocks, he is perfectly placed to enter her from above. Particularly deep thrusts are possible in this position, since her pelvis is tilted upwards, allowing for maximum penetration.

She can pull him more deeply into her by clutching his hips, and use her feet—if he likes that—to play with his nipples, chest, and neck, or have her toes sucked. It is easy to reach each other's bodies when making love this way and, although kissing is impossible, there's plenty of space for talking, laughing, and smiling. Her body in particular is more exposed than in the conventional missionary position, especially her breasts and clitoris.

he kneels

She lies back with her buttocks on the edge of the bed, while he kneels on the floor in front of her. The bondage and SM (sadomasochism) possibilities of this position, along with those described previously and below, could include strapping her ankles together using cuffs, which she could then use to draw his head towards her; or else she could toy with his nipples and chest with her feet, while wearing heels.

the car hood

As a variation on the position above, she lies back with her legs in the air and her buttocks at the edge of a table, counter, or even the hood of a car, while he stands in front of her. This is great for taking sex outside the bedroom. If he is standing, he is especially free to position himself for maximum stimulation of her G-spot; and to grind and rotate his hips, moving his penis around inside her. This position can't be beaten for fast, opportunistic lovemaking. She is thrillingly open to him. However, she's also prone to being pushed backwards, and may feel vulnerable, so he should take care to hold on to her.

the wraparound

She lies on her back, with her arms and legs open. Rather than lying on top of her, he crouches above her. She wraps her arms and legs around his shoulders and back, pulling herself close around him, and him deeper into her. Pillows or cushions beneath her hips and back may lessen the strain in her arms and legs.

He may feel that his thrusting movement is limited as she clings to him, and he needs strong arms, legs, and back to support her weight. And, as both partners are using their hands for support, loving touch is precluded. However, lots of constant movement is possible with this position. The thrusting, rocking, and inevitable changes of angle ensure that his penis enjoys tip-to-root stimulation, while he is more likely to deliver some stimulating strokes to her G-spot than in conventional missionary sex.

girls on top

Girls, he'll love it if you take the lead in bed! Apart from being able to feast his eyes on your body as you sway above him, he'll appreciate knowing that you're setting a pace that pleases you.

ride 'em, cowgirl!

He lies on his back. She straddles him and slides herself down onto his erection. She uses her thighs to move up and down. Unless she has an athlete's thigh muscles, this position can get tiring quickly and can induce cramp. Some women don't enjoy the exposure involved in this position, while others relish the break from being the one underneath, or even being squashed.

Meanwhile, some men prefer to be in control of the pace of the thrusts while others can feel vulnerable that they will slip out and suffer an injury if she rises up too high. Most men, however, relish the sight of their partner's pleasure and her bouncing breasts, which their hands can reach and play with. He can also use his hands to guide the pace to one he prefers, if he wishes. Or, with his hands under her buttocks or on her hips, he can help to push her upwards if her legs tire. This position is great during pregnancy, to avoid squashing her womb. More generally, this is a fun position for exhibitionists, and it's perfect for showing off a new sexy or kinky garment or set of lingerie. He'll want a pillow behind his head or else his neck is bound to get sore from staring up at you.

bareback rider

Alternatively, you can try the above position, except with her facing the other way. He lies back and she squats over him, facing his feet, and slowly lowers herself onto his erect penis. She leans forwards, on her hands, and moves up and down. Or else she can lean back over his chest so that they are lying cheek-to-cheek, almost able to kiss, teasingly.

It can take a while for both partners to get comfortable in this position and, what's more, it offers little clitoral stimulation for her through penetration alone. If she's leaning forwards, he can't reach her clitoris, but she can stimulate it herself. There's little work here for the man; however, if the woman is leaning forwards, he is free to play with her buttocks, anus, and perineum. If she leans back, he can reach her

clitoris and breasts. When she's leaning forwards, there's an anonymity to this position in which both partners can let their fantasies run wild. If she's leaning backwards, on the other hand, the position is curiously intimate and novel. Either way, it's the only position that combines the thrill of rear-entry sex with the perfect fit of woman-on-top sex.

"X" hits the spot

He lies back on the bed, supported by pillows, with his legs apart, while she lowers herself onto his penis. Then she very slowly leans back until she's lying backwards at a similar angle to him, with her legs extended, either side of his shoulders. From above, the two of you should look like the letter "X."

Be careful! His penis will be in a new and strange position, its upper surface moving more firmly than usual against her pubic bone. Penetration will not be as deep as usual for him and, since the top of his glans curves away more than its underside, his penis is more likely than usual to pop out, painfully.

That said, you can both enjoy great eye contact, and penetration is very visible this way: you can both see the penis sliding in and out of the vagina—a big turn-on. Penetration feels unusual for both of you, and the sense of not being able to move much can actually be a real tease, rather than the frustration you might expect. You both have plenty of space, if either of you is likely to get claustrophobic, while a mirror on the ceiling will unleash any sleazy-motel fantasies!

scissors

He lies back on the bed or floor and she squats over him, facing his feet. She slowly lowers herself onto his erection. She then leans forward, extends her legs behind her and slowly rocks up and down on his penis. She can't lie still because the angle of her vagina around his penis would bend it too much. And this isn't the position for her if she's not confident about her bottom.

However, her weight bearing down on him creates an incredibly snug fit. She can squeeze his penis with her buttocks during intercourse to make penetration feel even deeper, and can grab onto his legs as he thrusts, to keep her balance. The more she shifts around, the more different parts of the penis and vagina can be stimulated. She can lean onto his thighs if she's worried about being too heavy for him. For a novel pleasure—either for him or for her—he can play with and suck on her toes during lovemaking.

the professional

He sits up on the bed with his legs drawn slightly towards him. Straddling him, she lowers herself onto his erection, wraps her arms around his neck to balance, and hooks both of her legs over his shoulders. A slow, rocking motion is bound to lead you both to pleasure.

If you find it hard to balance, try this position with him leaning back against the headboard. She'll need to be supple in order to keep her legs in place throughout your fun. If you both like vigorous thrusts, this won't be the one for you; however, it is very intimate—you're wrapped up in each other, and it's easy to talk and kiss throughout. It also combines deep penetration with access to her clitoris, and is gentle, sensual, and slow. He can kiss and stroke her legs throughout, so this position's great with a pair of sexy stockings or boots.

female missionary

He lies back while she climbs on top of him, facing forwards, supporting her weight on her forearms, her legs extended behind her. Moving her whole body up and down will massage his penis. She can press her legs together to increase clitoral stimulation, or fan them outwards, forcing her hips further onto his shaft.

This position won't work at all if there is a big difference in your heights, and while some men enjoy the tease of moving to her pace, others aren't so keen. However, this is one of the only woman-on-top positions where you're intimate enough to kiss and talk throughout. Both of you can enjoy skin-contact all over your bodies, and natural erogenous zones like the breasts are turned-on. His pubic bone will grind against her clit. She is free to stop the action for a second or two, to delay his coming. This is a great position for him to enjoy if he likes restraint during sex. Tie him up, or cuff his arms to the bedposts, and pleasure yourself on top of him!

a little on the side

The following positions don't require much effort, and are great for those times when you want to relax and be close, but both want a bit more than a cuddle. Sensual and slow, they're perfect for when you're both a little tired, for example after an evening out. Many couples enjoy side-by-side lovemaking, since both feel equal; neither of you is on top, and control of the speed and depth is shared evenly between you.

spoons

She lies on her side, and he snuggles up behind her. She draws her knees towards her chest, assuming a slightly fetal position, and opens her thighs as he tucks his knees behind her, entering her from the rear. Once he is thrusting inside, she can raise and lower her topmost leg for greater or lesser penetration.

Penetration can feel a little shallow for some couples, especially if their sizes vary greatly. However, it's a great opportunity for him to indulge the sensitive skin of her

ears, neck, and shoulders, whether kissing, nuzzling, or using his hands. He can whisper those horny stories or messages of love in her ear, and this position is perfect for intimate, sensuous sex. With her cradled in his arms, this position also suggests those traditional, protective, and protected male and female gender roles. You don't even have to move to float blissfully off to sleep afterwards.

Try cuffing or loosely tying your ankles to each other's to add a thrilling element of bondage into an otherwise safe and secure position.

the living bed

This position's perfect for al fresco sex in the sun. As she lies on top, she can soak up the rays. Alternatively, it's another one for that mirror on the ceiling. He lies on his back and she allows him to enter her, either by crouching onto him, facing his feet, or by lying straight back on top of him, facing upwards, to begin with; in this case his penis may need a helping hand to enter her.

The idea of this position is that she lies back luxuriously on top of him, in a variation of "spoons" described above. However, she can either rest her legs along his or to each side of his with her soles flat on the bed or floor; or even, for a particular twist, tuck her legs beneath her so that her feet are beneath her buttocks. Her thighs will ache quickly, but, for a short while at least, she'll be able to "bounce" a little, and exercise a little elastic control—not to the extent that he's worried about his penis popping out!

Penetration isn't especially deep but it's very effective, and this position is especially horny and visual: for him, there is extra pressure on the underside of his shaft, while she can experience her own hands together with his as they caress, tease, and pluck at her taut breasts, nipples, tummy, and open labia. If she tilts her head and leans back, she might even be able to kiss his lips, and can bring herself off with her fingers as quickly or as slowly as she likes.

He has total access to her breasts and clitoris, too, and this position will make him feel satisfied as he thrusts. He will find he can support her weight more naturally than he might think, and he can thrust for a long time in this position, especially if she's much lighter than him, providing a steady bedrock to the highs and lows of her arousal. This position is as intimate or as distant and fantasy-fueled as you like. Because she is facing away from him, and because the base of his penis is pushing against the back wall of her vagina, he'll feel the deliciously intimate contractions of her anus and perineum as she comes.

face-to-face

The simplest way to get into this position is to roll over onto your sides from a conventional missionary position with him on top, maintaining penetration as you go. Otherwise, you can try to achieve it by edging closer, face-to-face and on your sides, with her raising her uppermost leg to allow penetration.

Take care not to squash each other's thighs. This position doesn't allow much thrusting, and may frustrate some couples, although that remains true of side-by-side sex generally, so this is no exception. Although penetration may be shallow, not only does this position allow great intimacy, it requires it, since if either of you let go, you may end up rolling backwards when he slips out of her. Meanwhile, you can kiss, caress, and talk dirty to your hearts' content.

For the adventurous, try holding yourselves together at your stomachs if possible, with a wide belt or straps. Massage oil (and a surface you can clean afterwards) takes this position to new heights of sensation.

the "Y"

She lies on her side facing him, with one leg in the air and the other flat along the bed. His lower leg slides against her lower leg while her raised leg rests on his shoulder and he penetrates her from the side.

With thighs easily squashed and hip-bones easily bruised, this isn't an ideal position for making love on a hard floor. Balancing can be difficult, and he'll find it more natural to stab jerkily, and more of an effort to establish a steady rhythm. However, it is really visual and playful, and lets you reach towards each other and watch and gaze at each other. He has a great view of his shaft sliding in and out of her vagina, and you both have a visual feast in each other's face and body. He can also reach and play with her inner thighs.

This position can be playful and fun, especially if you both like the idea of messing around with a video camera, and because her legs are so wide apart, she is very open to him. He can really experiment with the strokes that feel best, from gentle, shallow penetration, to deep, powerful thrusts.

take your seats

Trying the following positions will show you that sitting down on the job isn't always the lazy option. Indulged in regularly, they would soon firm up your thighs! However, seated sex can add a new and naughty dimension to your lovemaking and makes for some quite outrageous situations.

the human chair

He sits on a chair with his legs together. She sits on his lap, facing away from him, and lowers herself backwards onto his penis. He is held down by her weight and so she must do most of the work, rocking and thrusting to maintain arousal.

His penis is at just the right angle to stimulate her G-spot, and both of you can reach her breasts, nipples, tummy, and clitoris. This position is fun, but tiring for her upper legs. By grinding her hips into his lap, burying his penis to the hilt, and moving in a circular motion, she can minimize some of that strain.

Since both of you are looking in the same direction, and she is so exposed, this is a great position if you are watching something that turns you both on, or are facing a full-length mirror. From this position, it couldn't be simpler to move to another, such as doggy-style (see page 76), so it makes for a novel way to start making love.

the hinge

He sits in a (well-made!) chair while she straddles him, her knees up, so they're level with and on either side of his chest, and the soles of her feet are flat on the seat, either side of his thighs and buttocks. She holds onto the back of the chair and pushes away with her feet, moving up and down on his penis. His hands are free to explore the whole of her body, from her shoulders and breasts to beneath her buttocks, while this position can be both intimate enough for you to ˙kiss and caress and vigorous enough for you to scream the house down.

She may feel that if she relaxes too far onto him, her body weight will feel heavy on his thighs and put him off. Over a longer time, her thighs may get too tired for her to come. He can help with this and can master the rate of her movements, by placing his hands on her waist or under her buttocks and gently guiding her. Her nipples are in the perfect position for him to nibble and suck as she bounces up and down. As well as being fun and intimate, this is a great position for a quickie—and all the better because it's probably not the one you first think of.

the vice

He sits on the floor with his legs extended in front of him. Gently, she inches into his lap and onto his penis, until she can settle her full weight on him and wrap her legs around his back. The couple sit facing each other, with their legs crossed or wrapped around each other's backs. In this position, you can slowly rock yourselves to orgasm, hugging, massaging, or scratching and tugging at each other's backs.

It can be hard to balance, but as long as you don't let go of each other, she's in control of the thrusting. However, the sensation of all her weight bearing down on him will compensate! She'll need to inch a good deal forward against his tummy if she's going to take him inside her to the hilt.

Using all her weight can make for massaging penetration. She may enjoy setting the pace and how deep she takes him, while he may enjoy doing less than he's used to. Because of the way her legs are spread, the skin around her clitoris is stretched thinner than usual and is extra-sensitive to the touch. Being so up close and personal, you'll find yourselves kissing and whispering to each other. She can reach between his legs and play with his scrotum, while he can reach her clit. If he's feeling strong, he can cross his ankles under -neath her buttocks, which playfully makes for a little more "spring."

fine and upstanding

For urgent, racy, must-be-now lovemaking, sex standing up is a favorite. It's not for everyday, and marathon sessions would soon tire both of you, but it can't be beaten for the occasional quickie.

the here and now

This is the position of choice when you just can't wait until you're next near a bedroom! And, especially if you're excited enough to tackle each other standing up in the first place, you can come relatively quickly this way.

She sits on a surface about the same height as his pelvis. He stands in front of her and unzips his fly or—to avoid a tell-tale "ring of confidence" from her arousal—drops his pants and underpants completely. As he penetrates her, she brings her feet around to the small of his back and wraps her legs around him.

This is great in the kitchen, garage, or after hours at the office, but if there's no available worktop or desk, you can make love up against the wall. This offers less support for both of you, and will require some strength on his part, with his hands beneath her buttocks.

The thrill of a quickie can accelerate the woman's sexual response, and she may come more quickly than usual. Alternatively, her body may not provide lubrication quickly enough to make for easy penetration, no matter how excited she is. In this case you might wish to try some lubrication if convenient, but otherwise, the point is to have fun, so do something else!

If her weight is supported by a worktop or bench, she can put all of her energy into reaching orgasm. It also gives him more opportunity to thrust than if he is supporting her.

Spontaneous though it feels, this position does require at least a little forethought. Unless you are in your own kitchen, it does require skirts, swimsuits, or other clothes from which you can both be easily liberated. Keeping your clothes on is sexy as well as advisable—sometimes, less is more. Wear clothes that can be pulled to one side, rather than requiring complete removal.

halfway up the stairs

She stands on the stairs, facing away from him and in an upwards direction. Standing behind her, he enters her. He'll find what follows easiest if he places one foot on the stair above his back foot, with the rear leg straighter than the one in front.

Once he is inside her as far as the base of his penis, he circles one arm around her belly and, with the other arm, takes hold of her leg, just below the knee, with the other. Carefully, she takes one leg off the stair, gradually allowing him to support her, stretching her vagina around his shaft. If she feels confident enough in his strength, she can raise her other foot too, as far as is comfortable, and reach her arms behind her to touch his hips when she feels he has her whole weight. This will shift her center of gravity backwards and upwards, putting more of her weight on his arm around her tummy and making it easier for him to hold her that way.

He needs to be pretty strong for this, and she needs to be supple. You will both tire easily, and you can expect to find this hard to maintain. One solution is to have lots of mutual pleasuring and foreplay first, so that you're both on the brink of orgasm before penetration takes place. The other is to try with the expectation of sinking gently onto the stairs in due course. As he puts her down, it is essential to let her lower her leg first. She can lean forwards and place her hands and/or head on a higher stair while he drops to one knee. This will be a lot less strenuous for the two of you.

This is a great position if she enjoys a feeling of total surrender during sex, while he'll feel strong and manly. It also gives a great view! If you have a mirror safely at hand, or are recording yourselves, this is a fun, sexy, and very visual option. Do it right and she'll feel as if she's pitching and rolling on the bow of a ship. Resting on the stairs, it can feel deliciously filthy, rude, and spontaneous!

standing ovation

He begins by kneeling (he may find this easiest when beginning on one knee), and she lowers herself onto his erection, facing towards him. As she does so, she wraps her legs around his hips and puts her arms around his neck. Cautiously, he rises until he is standing up, carrying her with him and beginning to bump and grind his hips as he does so.

Don't worry if you can't take more than a minute in this position. It's just a fun, spicy twist that you can use to reach a position that offers some support for her buttocks, such as a counter, as he tries to stay inside her all the while. This is a position that appeals to traditional gender roles, with the man taking charge; she will not be able to govern movement much and is dependent on his bouncing her up and down to move on his cock at all. One variation that gives her an element of control is if he stands with his back to a wall, a foot or so away from it. She then has a surface to push against with her feet.

This is a fun position that can make you both feel sexy—if you do sustain it long enough to come, there's enough skin-on-skin contact between you to make this extra-special.

coming from behind

If it's deep penetration and G-spot arousal you're after, rear-entry sex does it every time. Sex from behind can reach places other positions don't. The position of the G-spot isn't the same in every woman, so some experimentation may be worthwhile to find what works for you. However, some couples relish the fast, furious, and animalistic nature of rear-entry sex for its own sake. Some couples are put off by the impression that rear-entry sex is not as intimate as other positions, but then again, not being face-to-face is a great time to focus on your own physical sensations and wildest fantasies.

doggy-style

She kneels on all fours, either on her hands or elbows, her legs slightly parted. He kneels behind her, his thighs at right angles to his calves, which rest along the bed or floor. He penetrates her vagina from behind, holding onto her hips to push and pull her onto him in time with his thrusting, or to steady her and hold her still so that he can enter as far as the base of his penis.

This is an intense buzz for the man, and it's not uncommon for him to come quickly in this position. Some women find it impersonal, while others, by contrast, relish being taken this way—it depends entirely on the individual. If his penis is larger than normal, she may feel overwhelmed by the depth of penetration possible.

There are lots of good reasons why this is the most common rear-entry position. It's the most natural—literally, as it's the way most mammals have sex! The angle means that his penis is well placed to stroke backwards and forwards against her G-spot, on the front wall of her vagina. Girls, if you're not sure where your G-spot is, this can be a good way to find out. You can reach back with one hand and stroke your own clitoris as he thrusts.

While he has a great view of his penis pushing and pulling in and out of her vagina, she can move in time with his rhythm as he places his hands gently around her hips, trading off control with him and finding out precisely where the experience is at its most intense.

doggy-style, standing

She leans forward against a wall, or holds onto something such as a banister or railing. He gets behind her and bends his legs until he's low enough to penetrate her from the rear. Alternatively, she can bend far forwards, holding onto her ankles, or even onto his for support. His hands on her hips and buttocks can also help here.

This is fast, furious, and animalistic. With her legs slightly together, her closed buttocks act to increase the clutching effects of her vagina, making penetration tighter and stimulating her labia and inner thighs. For him, the feeling of her buttocks being closer together is as if her vagina were longer, and penetration deeper. He can feel as if his penis is reaching right inside her womb.

This is a great position for a short time, and very energetic. It can become difficult to balance, though. It is best to be near a variety of anchored fixtures you can safely grab hold of. Not all couples are ideally suited to this when it comes to their relative heights. In any case, it's best if he's fully erect before entering her, and he may or may not enjoy the sensation of having his penis pulled slightly downwards.

If she takes to this, she can reach behind her and grab his buttocks, pulling him as far as possible into her. With more movement, he can really see his penis sliding in and out of her, while she is free to fantasize, so this is a great position if you like the idea of anal sex but are a bit reluctant to try it.

a rush of blood to the head

This isn't for every day, but it's a novelty, and a bit of fun, that is actually easier than it sounds. She lies on her back on the bed or floor (a firm but somewhat padded surface is best) and puts her hands on her hips. With her elbows beneath her, she pushes up her hips and legs as if she's about to thrust her legs into the air like a gymnast or yogi. He kneels in front of her and, taking hold of her calves or ankles, places her legs on his shoulders so that her ankles are either side of his neck and her feet behind his head.

Penetration can be difficult if he doesn't enjoy angling his erection downwards. Once inside, though, the upper surface of his penis can press pleasurably on her G-spot. It requires you both to be a little supple.

The upside-down position makes the blood rush to her head, which can really increase the power of her orgasm if she comes this way. If you're both strong enough that he can let go of a leg, then he can reach her clitoris with one hand.

The unusual view for both partners is a special thrill, as she looks up at him while he sees her breasts falling upwards towards her head as they bounce, and her hair, if it's long, spread out on the bed. Her arms are free to move and pleasure her breasts. It looks especially great if she's shaved!

love comes from behind

This is a wonderfully intimate position that can really become part of regular, loving sex despite involving rear entry. She lies on her front on the bed and raises her buttocks towards him, pushing up slightly onto her knees as he settles himself above her, being careful not to put all his weight on her. She parts her legs and, supporting himself with his elbows or on his hands, he should be able to penetrate her. Reaching around with one hand to guide himself can help.

It is hard for her to access her clitoris in this position, and maintaining the height of her buttocks, pushing upwards to meet his thrusts, can be tiring. It's a good idea to put pillows or cushions beneath her belly to avoid this.

He may be able to reach her clitoris with one hand, reaching in front of one thigh. This is a great position if the man enjoys controlling the depth and pace of the action. She can hardly move, so it is great for a woman who likes to give up control.

Penetration is deep, tight, and may hit her G-spot. The movement his penis is causing may cause her clitoris to rub pleasantly against the pillows or bedding. Nicest of all, this is the one rear-entry position in which it's possible to be really intimate; he can caress her neck and face, kissing her ears, and whispering softly or talking filthily to her, and she to him.

If you'd like a bit of tough but tender man-in-charge fun, it's easy for him to access her buttocks, squeezing or spanking them with his hand or even a hairbrush, sex toy, or paddle. The contrast between this and the ability to share your responses, with your faces intimately close, can be truly explosive. It's also a great position for light bondage, especially on a bed with a suitable headboard or bedposts.

come together

Strike a pose and you will discover parts of yourself that you didn't know you had! Whinny coltishly; shuffle around on all fours; pout, be playful and daring; surprise your partner with a sexy strip; find novel uses for champagne, lip-balm, warm tea, ice cubes, and toothpaste; have sex outdoors as much as discretion and the law allows; make a joke out of a weird fetish and still get to have it your way. Your greatest sexual asset is your imagination. The more daring you are, the more you'll find you're guaranteed to make each other's mouths water! Here are some positions that will have you both forgetting what time it is. These are perfect for vacations or those extra-special occasions when you have a little time and are relaxed. Once you've mastered these two, they may become favorites and are more likely than most to have you both coming together!

for her pleasure

He lies back on the bed while she lowers herself gently onto his penis, facing his face, with her knees on either side of him. She draws her lower legs up so that her knees are parallel with her own chest, and on either side of his lower ribs. If she moves her hips, she will find the most comfortable position at which her clitoris is directly over his pubic bone. This is the position in which she's most likely to have multiple orgasms.

Gently, she rocks over him, moving her clitoris against him and concentrating on pleasuring that, despite his penis moving inside of her. He should do his best to hold back from coming until she has had an orgasm. If she's able to come again, then keep going! If she is ready to stop and he is ready to come, she can masturbate him to orgasm or go down on him. Alternatively, for probably the finest experience, perhaps he can control himself enough to hold off but then let go when he feels she is on the edge of orgasm.

If the woman wants to come more than once, she's going to have to work for it, as this technique takes some practice to get right. But it's worth it! In addition to having his penis inside her, she has full body contact (her breasts are against his chest), and she is able to grind her clitoris against the firmness of his pubic bone in just the way she chooses.

Because he can't thrust, she can control the movement to just the right pace, while he can relax, enjoy, and know she is having a good time. By moving her legs, she can alter the depth and angle of his penis inside her vagina, making it possible to hit her G-spot. If you're feeling adventurous, a cock-ring for him, with some sort of clitoral stimulation attached, could be just the thing to give her some rewarding play.

snakes

This is another great position in which you're very likely to come together! The aim is to move at the same pace in the same way: it is based on pressing and rocking techniques rather than the thrusting we're used to. He is on top of her with his knees together against the bed, not dissimilar to the missionary position, but with his pelvis directly above hers.

Instead of thrusting from beneath, his penis straight, his penis is curved, and his hips are riding high. His penis is inside her, but its base is just outside her vagina, and his pubic bone is pressing down on her pubic mound. She wraps her legs around his thighs and rests her ankles on the backs of his legs. Keeping their arms and legs still, they push into each other at precisely the same rate and speed.

This depends on a rolling and rocking motion rather than thrusting in and out, in the way we've all become used to making love. Be patient, however, and this can be a real treat for her as her clitoris presses against him; he will enjoy the teasing delay while being very sensitive to the orgasmic contractions of her vagina. This position delays male orgasm, increasing the likelihood of your coming together.

showing some cheek

the highs and lows of anal sex

Some people, once they try it, take to anal sex, while others are understandably squeamish. It has a tough and transgressive image, but in fact anal sex can sometimes be surprisingly gradual, gentle, and shallow. Women who enjoy anal sex say they like the sensation of the filling snugness it provides, while, contrary to the clichés, not all gay men enjoy or prioritize anal sex.

Anal sex always requires lubrication. Unlike a vagina, the anus produces no natural juices. Don't use an oil-based lubricant, and always use extra-strong condoms since anal sex can make even those with a clean bill of health more vulnerable to infection. And, needless to say, don't put a penis anywhere near a vagina after anal penetration, without a wash as well as a change of condom.

solid as a rock

One of the lessons of gay male sex is that you can enjoy anal penetration along with face-to-face contact. She lies on her back, with her buttocks on the edge of the bed and her knees raised to her chest. A couple of pillows under her pelvis will adjust her to the right height for him. He stands, his legs slightly bent, and penetrates her, clutching her thighs as necessary for balance.

This position offers eye-to-eye communication, and she can control the degree of penetration by bringing her legs to her breasts, or wrapping them around him for a new and strange sense of intimacy. There's plenty of room for you both to play with her vagina and clitoris, too, for a potentially explosive all-over set of genital sensations.

the cradle

This position isn't face-to-face but it's no less intimate for that. She lies on her side on the bed in a fetal position, with her knees drawn up to her chest. He nuzzles her back and penetrates her. He's liable to squash his partner's thighs, and it's hard for him to build up a regular, deep thrust. You may both be a little frustrated by the limited movement that's possible in this position, although if he can place the soles of his feet against a wall or headboard, that may give him a little leverage.

Equally, the cosiness and limited movement of this position may make it less daunting. Both of you can reach her clitoris, while he can play with her breasts. Squeezing her buttocks together will squeeze the base of his penis, while moving her knees towards and away from her chest will deepen or lessen the depth of his penetration by lengthening or shortening her rectal passage, so she has a good degree of control. He can hold her, talk softly in her ear, and caress her from her hips to her hair. Assuming this position in front of a mirror will make you both feel even more intimate.

hidden shallows

She lies on her stomach on the bed, spreading her legs, with a couple of pillows under her pelvis to raise her buttocks. He penetrates her from behind, supporting his body-weight with his arms, his legs inside hers.

She won't be able to reach her clitoris, but otherwise this is a woman-pleasing position that is commendably shallow, so she will accommodate him more easily, especially if he is well endowed.

This sweaty, sexy position holds plenty of opportunity for skin contact—her nipples, breasts, and tummy are rubbed against the bed, while his nipples and chest are rubbed against her.

porn stars

This is the wildest and most downright animalistic anal sex position! She bends from a standing position, supporting herself against a surface, while her partner stands behind her and penetrates her from the rear, balancing them both by holding onto her thighs or playfully slapping and spanking her exposed buttocks.

If she relishes feeling dominated, and you both enjoy a sense of depravity, this will do! Otherwise it can feel out of control. Penetration can be deep, especially if he's apt to get carried away. He'll do well to control his thrusts, stay aware of how she feels, and not get lost in fantasy.

There is no shame in giving this position a wide berth: it can easily go beyond many people's limits. But if she has a taste for anal sex to begin with, then penetration is quick and easy this way as her anus is exposed, taut, and angled well. Because she is leaning against something, she can offer some resistance to his thrusts, while trying this over a securely fitted banister will make your heads spin!

dark places

bringing your innermost fantasies to the bedroom

Fantasy plays a big role in our lives. If we didn't dream of winning the Lottery, none of us would play it, and the things that we aspire to form a big part of our idea of who we are. Our fantasies drive us to achieve the kinds of lives we think we want for ourselves.

However, our sexual fantasies function a little differently, and because of this we shouldn't be scared of them. That's because, unlike other kinds of fantasy, sexual fantasies are not always, in fact, things we would really like to do!

We fantasize when we masturbate, replaying images of situations and lovers, real and imagined. Most of us use our imaginations to help us come by ourselves, and many of us fantasize in our own heads to turn ourselves on when we're making love. Many things occur to us in fantasy that we wouldn't try to make happen in reality, for one good prohibitive reason or another.

Group sex, all sorts of kinky sex from playful messy love to your darkest scenarios, gay sex, anonymous sex—any and all of these are commonplace sexual fantasies, and they're all normal. If you are ashamed of your sexual fantasies, it may help to know that psychoanalysts believe that shame is an inverted form of narcissism. Humankind is a strange and complex species: the chances are that the things that arouse you are probably not statistically that unusual for fantasies.

If you dream of success in a particular career, you will put up with the setbacks and inconveniences required to get there. These could involve extra training, anti-social working hours, commuting, and taking your boss seriously. Even the most committed SMer, however, would agree that it's not ideal to let your sexual fantasies rule your life in a similar way. Even though seeking sexual fulfillment is a goal in life for most, it shouldn't have to come at the cost of personal inconvenience, abusive relationships, and compromise of personal ambition.

Part of the nature of fantasies is that, by definition, they always go our way! Real life doesn't, and most of us don't need to be told the difference between fantasy and reality. Part of letting your sexual fantasies "know their place" is being able to discuss them with your partner. That might be a horrifying prospect for some, but you don't have to tell them everything, and you can bet that whatever's going on in your head, something equally rude and naughty is going on in theirs! Some people see a

partner's sexual fantasies as competition, and feel that their lover should be thinking of them. However natural, it's unrealistic! Far better to become a part of each other's fantasies, thanks to confident, unguarded lovemaking. If you talk about your fantasies in the right way, it can make for sizzling sex—either if you decide to act them out, or even just by sharing them. Simply knowing what your partner might be thinking about during sex is incredibly arousing by itself.

With enough closeness and intimacy between you, you can talk dirty, ask questions, and feel comfortable enough with each other to swap those filthy words and phrases that you've found are bound to arouse you and your partner. If and when you're trusting enough that the other will be receptive and kind towards your fantasies, you'll find that some can be acted out with a minimum of effort and preparation—al fresco or anal sex, for example—and all that it takes to find them out is a little frank and open conversation.

Some favorite female fantasies:

An anonymous encounter with a stranger

Sex with a regular partner

Sex with a friend, celebrity, or co-worker

Lesbian sex

Forced sex

Being watched

Being tied up or restrained

Watching another couple

A threesome with two men

Knowing exhibitionism

Some favorite male fantasies:

A threesome with two women

Sex with an anonymous woman

Dominating a woman

An erotic episode with another man

Anal sex with a woman

Being restrained or tied up

Group sex, watching and being watched

Sex with a prostitute

Viewing his lover make love with another man

Being dominated

swing when you're winning

Relatively few people who have fantasies of group sex actually act on them. While the idea of making love with more than one other person is a big turn-on, making it a reality can be fraught with difficulty. For those who do, however, the fact that society favors monogamy and frowns on swinging is itself arousing. Group sex is defined as more than two people indulging in sexual activity, but not necessarily involving penetration or even body-contact among all participants: for some, watching is enough. Evidence suggests that a surprisingly large number of people have had at least one experience of group sex of this kind.

In Europe and the USA, established swinging opportunities exist alongside the fetish scene, which is similar but less nightclub-based. Most people who indulge in group sex on an occasional basis do so with the participation of their partner, and have found that it brings a continued vibrancy, trust, and celebratory quality to their relationship. These are the lucky ones who have found that they can negotiate—either naturally or with a little work—the many natural jealousies that can occur around sex when more than the two of you are involved.

To do this, both people must be equally keen. You will not have a pleasant group-sex experience if you are not as enamored of the idea as your partner, but are trying to keep them happy. If you are naturally possessive and are wildly, passionately in love, you might find the fantasy image of watching your partner roll around with another lover incredibly arousing. Make sure that the real-life image will make you feel the same way.

As we all know, occasionally in life, events take care of themselves: a fun, joyful experience with no complications or caveats can simply happen to us while we experience it, while in reality it could not have happened if we had not been open and trusting enough. Otherwise, the various swinging opportunities that exist can be found through clubs, contact magazines, the Internet, and even a few specialized hotels. Most of these are couples-only, by-invitation affairs that require some form of informal vetting, and have their own language of abbreviations and acronyms for particular preferences.

Other people look for group-sex experiences when they are single. In the 1970s heyday of swinging in the USA, they might have done so by visiting "blue" hotels and motels. These days, some beauty spots and "lovers' lanes" have become commonly known within their localities as places where group sex takes place; in Britain this is known as "dogging," and only here may single men may be accepted as participants, or more usually, simply as viewers, with a brief and furtive gesture of consent. Care for personal safety, for public decency, and for the legality of the practice in your jurisdiction should always be taken with any kind of anonymous sexual experience.

However "dicey," these experiences are unlikely to be ones of emotional complexity. By contrast, group-sex with other couples will involve not only jealousy but the possible loss of anonymity and privacy, and the inevitable establishment of new and complex relationships. For some, this very aspect of risk contributes to the thrill of living "on the edge," while others more simply get off on the idea of watching, being watched, and the sensations of unfamiliar touch. The lucky few find their love of their partner immeasurably confirmed by the sight of them with a third person, as they see their lover anew.

In reality, group sex can be a complex experience in which the individual is very fragile. Most couples find it keeps its appeal best as a fantasy—if you want a hint of the excitement of group sex without taking on the emotional complexities swinging can involve, then there are plenty of pornographic videos you might both enjoy, which feature "a cast of thousands."

fetish frolics

You name it, someone somewhere is sexually aroused by it. All kinds of surprising objects and habits turn people on, and intimate, self-determined pleasures are a sign of psychological complexity and a product of human evolution. There are websites devoted to all sorts of fetishes and physical accouterments, such as medical neck and body braces, while some people even take a harmless private pleasure in seeing others spit in the street! Fetishes can be puzzling, but not always troubling, and we don't always feel the need to understand them.

Sigmund Freud wrongly came up with the idea that sexual fetishes are a result of castration anxiety. Among the incorrect conclusions this led to was the idea that only men can be fetishists. Any visit to a fetish club will reveal the lie in that.

Meanwhile, fetishists themselves are hard pressed to explain why they enjoy the things they do. They feel it's reductive to try to do so, and reject the implication that sexual fetishism is infantile. Only an average number of people who enjoy the look and feel of rubber or PVC, for example, were made to sleep on plastic sheets or had a childhood problem with bedwetting.

Freud believed that a fetishist could not be happy being the way they were: that because of the weird nature of what they liked, they must not be in control of their desires, and must be acting compulsively, uncontrollably. Therefore he used the word "fetish" (a Portuguese word for a religious icon without which African peoples could not worship) to suggest that "fetishists" could not become aroused without their fetish object.

These days, we'd call people who are unhappy with their sexual selves, or who feel driven to non-consensual or abusive acts, paraphiliacs. Self-identified sexual fetishists, meanwhile, are averagely well-balanced people, generally as in control of their sexual desires as anyone else. They may have found that they prefer making love in a certain way, but that doesn't mean it's the only way they can become aroused.

We are all fetishists in the sense that the psychological mechanism of arousal is the same, whatever turns us on. Stockings and garter belts are staples of male sexual fantasy, but they're not always thought of as fetish objects. Many men find the idea of a woman taking off a pair of glasses, or unpinning and shaking down her hair highly arousing—on which view, that becomes fetishistic behavior.

People of both sexes love the sight of their partner in a well-tailored suit, that hugs and falls away from the body in just the right way—another everyday fetish, while silks and satins have always been favorite fetish materials from before the commonplace use of leather and rubber. These effect a second skin that shimmers in the same way as PVC does in the eyes of a modern-day fetishist. As the English Restoration poet, Robert Herrick, wrote:

> *Whenas in silks my Julia goes*
> *Then, then, methinks how sweetly flows*
> *The liquifaction of her clothes.*

So even back in the seventeenth century, people were writing fetish poems. While there are many for whom the idea of being a member of a perverted sexual subculture is part of the thrill, many of our fetishes are so acceptable that we don't generally think of them as such.

Meanwhile, throughout the history of fashion, fetish styles have come and gone. From the 1970s to the 1990s, many haute couture designers, from Karl Lagerfeld to Thierry Mugler, have adopted elements of fetish fashion and used leather and rubber extensively, while debate raged about whether fetish elements such as corsets and high heels turned their wearers into empowered modern women expressing their sexuality and feeling gorgeous, or slaves to fashion. Madonna, wearing Jean Paul Gaultier's basques and conical bras, brought these styles to the stage.

Much fetish style is inspired by role-play scenarios and images from culture that have become sexually loaded. This is where fetishism overlaps with SM practices. You may have always been titillated at the thought of being a housemaid, a naughty nurse, a burlesque go-go dancer in a feather boa with "pasties" covering your nipples, or a dashing highwayman—characters you can not only dress up as but have fun with, pastiching every Hollywood or comedy cliché. Go on to make love in character as much as you wish!

fantasies and foreplay

Of course, there are hardcore sexual hobbyists who enjoy marginal practices such as corporal punishment or human pony-carting as ends in themselves, and are more likely to base not only their intimate sexual lives but some aspects of their social lives around their favorite interests, too. For them, whether or not a session or scene ends with intercourse is secondary to the opportunity to indulge their kink in the first place; then to go away and think about it later.

For the rest of us, some degree of kinky sex has become an increasingly accepted part of foreplay, and big business for some. Erotic retailers commonly sell affordable versions of high-class fetish toys and sex-wear, and references to kinky sex are a dime a dozen in popular culture. Nonetheless, that doesn't mean we should take it for granted that a partner won't be freaked out or "fazed" by something we'd like to try—subtle and sensible negotiation beforehand is essential.

Fetishism, restraint, and erotic pain—involving varying degrees of remaining playfully "in character," or being your truest self—all overlap in various ways that are too socially complex for the scope of this book, except to point out the psychological and practical cautionary points of safe, sane, and consensual behavior that are made in Safe, Sane, and Consensual (pages 118–125). Some people are uncomfortable with the extent to which sadomasochism resembles real abuse, even though it's fairer to say that it mocks it. It still remains less emotive for advertisers and the media to represent kinky behavior with an image of a woman dominating a man, rather than vice versa, for example.

Nonetheless, an understanding that there's a difference between fantasy and reality, and that not all fantasies—even those we act out—are actually things we'd like to have happen for real, is commonly held these days. While a minority choose to adhere to a demanding SM lifestyle full-time, this understanding frees the majority of us to enjoy the submissive and dominant aspects of our sexuality, and swap these roles (which is known to SMers as "switching") without worrying that we're reinforcing traditional gender roles or introducing new forms of oppression.

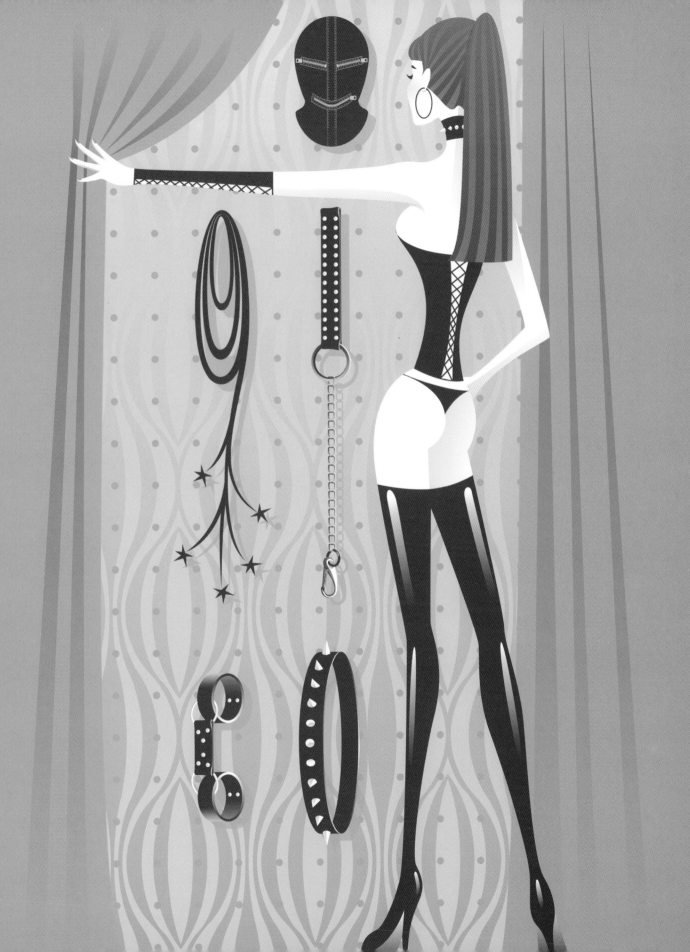

role-play

If this is new territory for you, the following fun, fetish ideas might be just the thing to spark your curiosity. Playing out a "scene" and assuming characters during sex doesn't mean you're not interested in who each other really is; quite the opposite, as your partner may also be getting in touch with parts of themselves they didn't know existed.

Develop as much of a storyline as you like. You might not feel you'll be able to keep a straight face, but then again, humor can be an essential safety valve and saving grace during kinky sex, in which powerful feelings can sometimes come to the fore unexpectedly. If you're both equally keen, then set aside some time to really indulge your fantasies—days off, evenings, weekends—when worldly worries are least likely to intrude and you won't watch the clock. Plan ahead, thinking carefully through details, plots, and accessories.

- Many magazine articles recommend making a date with each other and pretending to be strangers as a way of putting the spark back in your relationship; but have you ever thought of doing it not as a remedial treatment but as a bit of fun? It's a good starting point for the very act of pretending that things are different from usual.
- If you're interested in power and submission, think about exploring them with your partner. What sexual positions would give you or a partner a feeling of surrender? What words or attitude from you would give them a thrill to obey or control? Think about the literal roles that you could play—not all of them costumed or that out of the everyday—that would give a context to these feelings.
- Strip seductively for him. The more clothes you have on, the more you'll be able to tease him, while straps, belts, and buckles are similarly all opportunities to delay proceedings! So when you think about what to put on beforehand, remember that some clothing is often sexier than nakedness. Set a scene, with lower lighting than usual, and remember to dress—especially when it comes to undies and garter belts—in reverse order to how you will undress.
- Being away from home together is a tonic for any relationship, and why not think about the role-play possibilities your new, temporary environment affords? Hotel rooms often have a sense of corporate anonymity that might fuel a paid-for fantasy of businessman and call-girl, while others have a whiff of a sleazy motel, full of possibilities. Or, if you're lucky enough, your suite might make you feel like a duchess and her manservant on a grand tour!

• If you're playing the dominant or dominatrix, think about what it takes to be good at it: be measured, smooth, and don't deliver your partner any nasty surprises, especially if you're playing with erotic pain (see pages 106–107); nothing will spoil an edgy, arousing scenario faster than an inept move that hurts in a way that wasn't intended or expected. Get into your role, but don't get carried away. Remember that you're hoping to satisfy your partner's needs, and gain their approval in a way that means it's you who's really being submissive!

• Don't overlook the role-play possibilities of the rooms in your home. Boss and employee is a popular basis for fantasies. If you have a home office or study, you don't have to risk sneaking your partner into your workplace after hours.

• Try going through each other's wardrobes. Even if cross-dressing strikes you as something you'd never pull off, why not see what you'd look like in each other's clothes? She might look bold, assertive or androgynous in one of his suits, while for him the early moments of transformation can be a revelation! The strange feeling of the other sex's clothing will be an insight in itself.

• Doctor and patient are role-play favorites, while the naughty nurse has been a cultural figure for years. Medical scenes offer opportunities to touch, taste, and smell materials we don't always surround ourselves with during sex, and they're a perfect opportunity for a little fearful anticipation and playful control, too. You don't have to get too exploratory in order to play with contrasting sensations and temperatures. Uniforms, toy stethoscopes, plastic sheeting, and disposable rubber gloves—to give your hands that alien, clinical feel—are all affordably available. Surprise and tease your partner, being sure, for the greatest effect, to keep your voice and movements cool, measured, and clinical at all times.

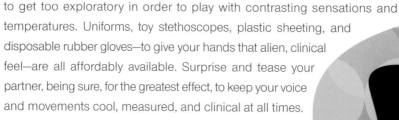

• The figure-hugging sportswear, sweat, exertion, and power relationships of sport are quietly spoken fetishes that turn a lot of people on. Playing at being personal trainer and athlete is tailor-made for power-play fun.

plastic clubtastic

Politician and intern, master and servant, saint and sinner, police and miscreant—if you've found whatever it is that turns you both on, think of the extra thrill of adopting those appearances in the presence of other people. Of course, you may be completely daunted by the idea, but what about the possibility of you and your partner visiting a fetish club? As foreplay goes, going out makes a change from staying in! The reasons to be fearful go away if you make the right choice of place: they should be, and usually are: utterly consensual and without pressure; female-friendly/dominant; relaxing; not full of dauntingly beautiful people; surprisingly uncritical of appearance for somewhere whose theme is sex; and full of a range of age groups.

Unlike swinging clubs (see pages 92–93), people's aim is not necessarily to have sex on the premises, and the emphasis is on having a sense of playfulness, perhaps by remaining in character. You can act out your doctor-and-patient fantasy, or spend the evening nursing drinks. The established club codes are easily learned, and "no" always means "no."

Although dress codes can be "strict," you don't always have to spend a fortune as long as you make an effort, so that other club-goers can feel that everyone's joined in the spirit of the evening—a visit to an army-surplus store, for example, could cheaply furnish two of you with a military theme. You'll find that reputable clubs in Europe and the USA will have a smoothly corporate image, a professional attitude to responding to inquiries, and welcome newcomers—they're businesses, after all—and are easily located. So if anywhere gives you a secretive attitude, move on. Apart from the Internet, an established local adult shop should have details of reputable clubs and fliers for upcoming fetish events in your area. If you go, you'll be sure to get in a cab bound for home with heads full of erotic possibilities!

sub-culture

bound to please

Bondage is the activity of restraining and being restrained during sex. It can be performed as part of penetrative or non-penetrative lovemaking, or as an end in itself, and it can be carried out either as part of sub-dom role-play, or with both of you on an equal and everyday relationship footing, for sensation alone rather than head-games.

Needless to say, trust—not just practical but emotional—is essential, and there are caveats to observe (see pages 120–125) that apply to bondage and corporal punishment equally. Dark stuff aside, the partner in restraint will know the experience is being created almost purely for them. It is essential that their temperament and pre-existing sexual fantasies already predispose them to some degree of sexual submission, and if they are predisposed, then fulfillment can be unspeakably delicious.

Some people are clearly aware which side of the dominant or submissive divide they are drawn to. If, however, you feel a bit kinky but can't decide, then evidence suggests you fall into the psychologically largest group. It's natural to "switch" and explore your options—if you can't decide, then you don't have to. Some kinky people settle down to their favorite practices after a while; others spend a lifetime having fun trying to find out.

If it's your turn in the dominant role, then be restrained—it's really you who is serving your partner's needs. In dominating them you are giving to them, leading them down a path of experience in a similar spirit to how you might give a massage. If you push boundaries, it should always be to your lover's pleasure.

Many find the fantasy of helplessness and immobility relaxing—it removes the background stress of decision-making to which we are usually subject all the time. Rope bondage has many devotees and is a highly evolved science (see page 124), while more information on the wide variety of purpose-made bondage toys is given in Sex and Shopping (pages 108–117). A little investment here can be the best of all options, as purpose-made cuffs and clamps are the most comfortable of all options, especially if your dominant partner has not been practicing techniques for years. Buckles and catches are simple and, on most properly designed devices, not reachable by the wearer. They are easily applied and, more importantly, are easy to achieve quick release from if necessary.

If you can't help feeling that all this "master and servant" stuff is just too stilted and you keep giggling, then why not try a more spontaneous approach to bondage, involving strength games. To avoid the terribly formal approach, wrestle and tickle your partner into submission—or try your best but find yourself on the losing side!

Here are a few ideas involving bondage or role-play that will have dominants puffing up their chests and submissives sulking.

• When out in public, having the sub carry the dom's bags, asking permission to use the bathroom, or performing any other acts of obedience that others don't have to know are part of a private code, will have you both thinking of what will happen when you're somewhere private again!

• Safe-words aside (see page 120), the sub doesn't speak unless spoken to, and addresses the dom as "Master" or "Mistress," "Madam" or "Sir" at all times.

• Closets, cupboards, and woodsheds all make temporary places of confinement for the disobedient submissive. Be sure to taunt and tease them as you stand guard.

• Assuming positions, including stress positions—hands on head, for example—is a humiliating alternative to being restrained.

• Cuff or strap your submissive to a secure point by one wrist, so that objects of desire—drink, snacks, cigarette—are tantalizingly just out of reach of the other hand.

going for the burn

To interpret pain as pleasure is a sign of how aroused you are. People who enjoy SM and erotic pain do so because they interpret pain differently when they're in a state of sexual arousal. Many of us have woken up in the morning with marks we don't remember being made the night before, and SM works on the same principle. Hardcore fans of SM view these marks as the physical trophies of how sexually carried away they've been.

"Punishment" can vary from sustained form of pressure such as nipple-clamps, to CP (corporal punishment) and light spanking. Light SM can still be psychologically loaded, enforcing dominant and submissive roles, even if it's not very painful. While precautions apply (see pages 118–125), SM in the right hands can feed your bodies' arousal just as fantasies feed your minds'.

Sometimes erotic pain answers a psychological need, the recipient getting off on the pain as part of their absolute surrender, and sometimes physical sensation leads to arousal by mimicking it: blood rushes to the surface of the skin; we cry out; our bodies release endorphins that have an anaesthetic effect; we can experience a similarly powerful reaction. This can be a factor in whether one prefers harder or softer chastisement.

People who enjoy the scenarios and style of SM as much as pain itself find that the sounds it—and they—create make a large contribution to their arousal. Dominants enjoy the sight of their partner's buttocks or other intimate places reddening, but a smooth dom doesn't rupture the skin.

Remember that SM can affect different people in differing and surprising ways. Feelings may surface that neither of you expected—be sensitive to each other and prepared for that. A combination of SM and bondage can be especially powerful. Many CP scenarios do not involve restraint, and you may prefer to experiment with each separately before mixing the two in more hardcore ways.

When it comes to repeated smacks from a hand or instrument, start gently and build up, choosing only your partner's fleshiest places. The gentler the skin is treated at first, the more desensitized it will be to harder strokes as you progress. Remember not to take your partner by surprise, by varying the placing and timing of your strokes, spanks, or slaps wildly or unexpectedly. Resting your hand or device on your target for a second before raising it for your stroke will give your sub an idea of what to expect, which is necessary for them to enjoy themselves.

Remember that if you are using an instrument such as a crop, cane, paddle, or even a whip, you will be removed from the sensation of pain yourself, and it's easier to get carried away. A hand-spanking—with the flat of the palm—is best administered with the wrist loose and the fingers and thumb held relaxed in a line. Arching your fingertips back slightly makes for a tidier impact, while letting your finger-ends impact a fraction of a second after your palm makes for an extra sting! You will know precisely how much pain you are dishing out because your palm will start to sting increasingly, too. For the tender-hearted "dom," this is an empathetic way to administer CP.

The context in which pain is dished out varies uniquely. Many submissive people find that a sub-dom scenario has the advantage of letting them "invite" their punishment of choice by "misbehaving," which is more arousing and erotic than having to ask outright for it. Whatever your pleasure, SM sex can sometimes be overwhelming. It can also bring you unspeakably close. Either way, be sure to cuddle, cradle, and reassure each other afterwards.

sex and shopping

Most of us are ready to take the weight off of our feet after shopping, but the following chapter will give you a host of new, different, and far saucier reasons to do the same thing! Whether you return home with a feather boa, furry handcuffs, or fetishwear, a trip to the bedroom might be in order if you add some of the following ideas to your shopping list...

clothes and toys

Sex-related products have moved from the back streets to the main street. *Sex and the City* established that chic urban women are interested in sex, too, and in recent years, high-rent shopping areas have seen the effects of their spending power. European and American cities now commonly feature female-friendly sex stores, that endeavor to be a little more fashion-aware than the bead-curtained retail outlets of old, which often put a burlesque spin on making women feel sexy.

The last few years have also seen the growth of a small but exclusive sex-product market. Custom-made kinky equipment; high-quality boned corsetry; and elaborate luxury dildos and vibrators have all made column inches in women's magazines. Many major cities even have one or two stores that specialize solely in vibrators or condoms.

Clothes themselves can be a great way for us to express ourselves, especially when it comes to sexual assertiveness, and just because they're sex-related doesn't mean they have to be cheap, tacky, and solely man-pleasing anymore. In fact, it's not just fetishists who feel that flesh is best covered up. Most of us agree that nakedness isn't everything—that clothes can frame and enhance our bodies sexily, either for foreplay or for sex itself, and feel great and extra-stimulating to wear, too. There's something highly erotic and teasing about not being able to see everything—either at the start of lovemaking, or throughout.

Be true to yourself in your choice of lingerie, and treat yourself to an exaggerated version of the kind of underwear you prefer already: if you're an action-girl who prefers sporty underwear, then go for clingy or sequined versions of the Lycra-based garments you might ordinarily wear, rather than feeling you have to impersonate a French whore. This goes for men, too. A glance at the willowy male models in any style magazine will show you that there's a range of flattering and slick but comfortable products out there, whether you prefer briefs or boxers. No longer is male sex-wear restricted to those terrible novelty posing pouches, so there's no excuse for dressing up for an evening out, only to get your partner home and drop your trousers to reveal brown nylon.

Corsets have long been a subject of debate as to whether they symbolize the empowerment or enslavement of women. They're associated with Victorian oppression, and yet women who love them claim to feel securely held at the waist, with their shoulders forced back, giving them an Amazonian confidence. A corset and heels can suggest a submissive moppet or an imperious dominatrix. Leave tight-lacing to the body-modifiers. A front-fastening corset as pioneered by Vivienne Westwood is something you can slip in and out of sexily as the mood takes you, without needing ladies' maids to lace you and a bedpost to grab hold of!

color choice

Black Suggests sophistication, experience, and SM play.

Red Speaks for itself. Traditionally the color with which prostitutes would advertise themselves, it will reduce most men to gibbering wrecks.

White Makes for virginal, vanilla fun. Put it on and let yourself be corrupted.

Silver and gold Suggest a special occasion, and puts glitz on your hips. An out-of-the-ordinary choice for a sexy strip.

Pewter Flatters the flesh of most ethnicities wonderfully.

material options

Lace An age-old sexy option, which gives teasing glimpses of the flesh on its other side, while its ticklish effects can prepare you for your lover's touch.

Silk Sensual, classy, and clinging. It can be worn under other clothes for a private turn-on. This most romantic of fabrics doesn't have to be confined to your clothes, either. Although it's expensive, try it for your bedding, too.

Feathers They feel fabulous. They're teasing to the touch, so join the burlesque revival.

Latex There's a range of fetishwear to suit all pockets—from cheap, wet-look latex that will turn you on until you tear it, to the classiest Italian Napa leather. But if you fancy yourself as a fetish fashion designer, or for a bizarre turn-on for your partner, try some tubs of liquid latex. Drip it on curves and watch it set in sensual designs.

Collars and chokers These are fashion items with a kinky history. They suggest a lover who can be controlled, but only those in the know will suspect the symbolism.

Many people try accessories with which they can beat their partner, only to find that the palm of their hand was best all along. That said, as props go, nothing reinforces your dominance more naturalistically than emphasizing your blandishments with an instrument of punishment. All of these are commonly available in your average sex stores.

Whips Although "whips and chains" is the lazy way we refer to kinky sex, whipping is probably a minority pursuit within the fetish community. Some would say the main assets of a whip are the caress it gives when wrapped in a hand, the light bondage you can achieve with it, the feeling as it trails across a body, and the things you can do with the handle. Whipping itself is heavy. It's more difficult than casting a fly, and requires practice by aiming at inanimate objects, such as pillows, first. They're foremost a style thing: the true secrets of the whip are little known outside of theatrical fighters and professional dominatrixes. Most of the whips we see come from joke and costume stores and are made of cheap, abrasive, and unsupple material. Don't use whips with weighted or knouted tips, unless they're tiny floggers or mini cats-o'-nine-tails. If you do attempt whipping, apply only quality leather to shoulders, buttocks, and—at a pinch—thighs, and on no account leave the kidneys and small of the back unprotected. Limit yourselves to a maximum of three whipstrokes, and make them the well-timed denouement of a cathartic scene.

Canes Canes are available as heavy rattan versions of old corporal punishment instruments. Avoid these in favour of shorter, lighter, cheaper "party" canes, which are far more useable—and quieter—in the bedroom.

Floggers Shorter bondage instruments include floggers and "pussy whips." Quality crops are easily available from either fetish or equestrian stores, and most affordable ones these days are made of insulated plastic. They're a pose, and much easier to wield and bear sustainedly than a whip. Canes and crops are both capable of mild, playful foreplay use. As with hand-spanking, remember to build gradually.

Paddles Paddles are useful tools that amplify the action of hand-spanking and are flat with a handle, like table-tennis paddles. Thanks to the appliance of science, some have holes in them to decrease wind-resistance on the downward stroke. They produce a more gradual, burning sensation than the slices of crops or canes, and so are easier to take over time. A tawse is similarly short but straighter, consisting of two split pieces and evil! Developed within the Scottish school system, they are still for sale on the fetish market.

a girl's best friend

Dildos and vibrators give you a new erotic charge whether you're with a partner or solo. These days, a visit to any sex store will reveal an eye-popping selection. Women have been using dildos since back in the cave, although back then they were flint or stone. Ironically, similar crystal or onyx dildos are available today at the more expensive stores, and are said to be great fun when warmed a little first.

Sex toys aren't just for singles, and aren't a rival to a real penis. Vibrators can massage her clitoris, other places, and him, too. Some people are deterred by the sound and fuss of a vibe, but you get what you pay for. More expensive ones are most adjustable and sound the least tinny. As if to emphasize their dual use, vibrators now come with clitoral or anal stimulators, while cock-rings for him can also provide clitoral stimulation. When it comes to strap-ons, leather ones are particularly popular because of their realistic feel. If she likes the sensation of being filled for much of the time, she might enjoy a short, flexible dildo placed inside such a strap.

Pleasure-balls (sometimes referred to as "Thai" balls) are not for anal use. Placed in the vagina, with lubrication, they are effective at toning your pelvic floor muscles, since you'll need to hold the balls in place in order to enjoy yourself. Some women report walking around on the edge of coming for as long as they like.

boys' toys

At the hardcore end, there is a variety of imprisoning "chastity" devices available for his cock and balls, which can be worn for a long time thanks to hygienic materials and the freedom to urinate. Denying a man his erectile arousal is a particularly frustrating torture! Left like this for some time, he'll be more than ready to perform. Many wrap around to fasten behind the testicles, raising and presenting them, too.

Cock-rings, meanwhile, are available in flexible rubber and, rolled to the base of the penis, are used to prolong an erection. Be careful, and do not go to the extreme lengths that male strippers do, using elastic bands that can be hard to remove and may damage tissue. Some cock-rings incorporate clitoral stimulators, which give them an added *raison d'etre*.

Anal toys such as butt plugs can be used, with lubrication, to relax an anal sphincter and stimulate the prostate. They come in a range of styles and sizes that vary in degrees of formidability. Anal toys should always be designed with a recessed ring above a widened base, to prevent the object being inserted too far.

tasty tidbits—sex and food

the naked chef

Food is a perennial precedent to lovemaking—there is something intimate about preparing and sharing food with your lover. Anthropologically, food is associated with intimacy since it's believed that kissing developed from the passing of food from one mouth to another.

It's not a great idea to eat large amounts of rich food before sex. Fish dishes and salads will leave you hungry for sex and nutritionally sated. Nonetheless, there's plenty of ways to mix food and fun.

- Little champagne bubbles popping against your skin is a tasty sensation, but the same feeling against your genital flesh is something not to be missed! If you don't drink alcohol, sparkling spring water will do just fine.
- Traditional aphrodisiacs earned their reputations because of how sexually suggestive they looked, felt, and tasted, as much as for any real properties: asparagus is a phallic vegetable and a sensuous feast, while oysters are moist and velvet, like a vagina, salty like semen, and have to be swallowed sensually.
- Ginger, fennel, and licorice are proven aphrodisiacs, while some spices will cause blood to flow to the genitals and bring a flush to the cheeks.
- Movable feasts: Have some messy fun on a plastic sheet: write your fantasies in food on each others' naked bodies; challenge your partner to lick off as much liquid chocolate as they can handle! Fans call this "splosh," and there's even a genre of colorful pornography devoted to it.
- Experiment with foods and temperatures, but avoid hot food, of course. Room-temperature to freezing is variety enough. Ice cream, fancy fruits, and honey all make a delicious feast of sexy fun. Trail them around each other's genitals as part of oral sex. Don't stick to sweet foods, either—all the old jokes about cucumbers are true! Remember, however, that not all foods taste as good as they are visually appealing, and unless you're playing with temperatures, give anything out of the fridge a chance to reach room-temperature first.

safe, sane, and consensual

Making your love lives a little more elaborate requires

a degree of care, but fortunately not a degree in it.

Absorb the contents of the following chapter,

and you can be reasonably sure that you

won't have missed any of the issues you should

have given thought to regarding safe sex,

SM, or bondage games. So read on,

and surprise your lover with your confidence.

Let your sexual self be all it can be!

the essential dos and don'ts of kinky sex

what's my motivation?

In consensual SM, the dominant is sometimes characterized as the instrument of the submissive's desire to punish themselves, or the sub as applying self-discipline with the aid of the dom. On this model, it's really the submissive's desires that triumph. At their best, SM and bondage are life-affirming experiences; but in some instances, it's not always easy to tell to what extent they drift towards forms of abuse, too. In heavy SM, more sensitive doms worry that their submissives could be deluding themselves that they are enjoying something that may seem unpleasant, and entering a "false consciousness." If you are uncomfortable with something you are being asked to do, because it seems painful, harmful, or too symbolically degrading, then sit down and discuss it with your partner even if you are the doer not the done to. Otherwise, by not being sure of your ground, you'll be mentally abusing yourself, too.

Sigmund Freud first identified sexual fantasies as the product of our own experiences. Psychologists still debate whether or not kinky desires are a product of personal conditioning, or just who we are. One thing that is clearer than it was in Freud's day, however, is that even if fetishism or SM is conditioned behavior, that doesn't mean it's beyond the kinky person's control—so don't be ashamed of those deepest, darkest desires. Early psychoanalysts believed that we were simply driven to repeat powerful experiences. The truth is rather that we actively and soundly desire to explore them, and that the meaningful boundaries we transgress are personal, not social ones. Kinky sex allows us to plan for the unplanned, do things we don't ordinarily do and be different to how we usually are.

Although it celebrates fun, kinky sex can make for times of emotional fragility. Live by the golden rule, and don't do to others what you wouldn't like to have done to yourself, by degrading or hurting them more than they have invited you to do. Fantasy and reality can differ, so discuss your fantasies before you enact them, thinking as you do of how you'll really feel. Humor and good negotiation of boundaries are essentials. Only consider pushing at your partner's limits when you are both in exactly the right mood in which it will enhance their pleasure.

While honesty is important, not all fantasies are for sharing, and no one has ordained that to have a good relationship you need to know everything about each other. Some private epiphanies shouldn't be dumped on a partner—that fantasy about their sister or brother, for example. Only share a fantasy if you think it will enrich the quality of your relationship.

the unbreakable rules of bondage and discipline

- If you have children living with you, remember to keep all accessories well out of sight at all times. Invest in a lockable trunk. Even though, as parents, we're all discreet, there are times when kinky sex couldn't be further from our minds, and it's then we're likely to forget.

- Bondage is fun only if you trust each other, which is why it becomes a staple of some long-term couples. If you must have kinky sex with someone you don't know all that well, tell a friend where you're going and tell them to call your cell phone. Keeping the prearranged time of the call to yourself, casually mention to your lover that you're expecting a call from your friend. A reasonable human with fun intentions won't bat an eyelid.

- The usual dating rules apply. Never have sex with someone you meet online unless you've gotten to know them face-to-face, too. If you're looking to find a partner with specific sexual interests, there may be the better alternative of going fetish clubbing with a friend, where you can check people out for as long as you like.

- Make sure you both clearly understand how far is too far. Agree on what you will and won't do beforehand. If you are going to indulge in role play where the submissive partner may "protest too much," make absolutely sure you have a safe-word or a phrase that really means no. Something utterly unconnected with sex is best.

- Alternatively, do what some hardcore SMers do and have a traffic-light system of red, yellow, and green; saying "yellow" allows the dom to lessen their activity without stopping altogether, saving face, if that's important to them, when they're about to go a bit too far. In return, they understand that "red" should bring them to an emergency stop.

- Maintain constant and honest communication about how you feel. Be aware of your breathing and heart-rate. If things take an odd psychological turn for you, if you feel nauseous, or just unsexy, don't be ashamed to bail.

- Make sure the sub can be released quickly, that knots are professional and buckles and catches are readily at hand. Imagine for a second what you would do and how quickly you could react if someone shouted "Fire!"

- If you have any health problems, speak up. Make sure you mention anything like a recurring bad back to your partner, let alone epilepsy or heart trouble. Don't indulge in breath-play if you have asthma or allergies, and stay aware during lengthier bondage games if you have a fatiguing condition such as M.E. If you are shy of mentioning something that you think could become an issue between you, or that you are personally embarrassed about, remember that your personal safety, along with a responsibility to your unsuspecting partner, is far more important.

- A playful spanking aside, don't play kinky games under the influence of mood-altering substances. Although sex, drugs, and rock 'n' roll go together when it comes to style, alcohol and drugs impair your judgement with regard to kinky sex, generally by making the talking easier and the doing more challenging. You may find yourself inept, out of your depth, or simply coming down and becoming more vulnerable, at the wrong time.

- Don't leave people alone in restraint, especially if any kind of gag or breath-play is involved. If it's part of a scene to abandon your lover, remember it's just pretend. Stand in the corner silently, in case their arousing panic becomes too real.

- Even in mild bondage positions, immobility can soon lead to cramp. In addition to making sure the sub can communicate and be released quickly, they should keep hydrated, drinking plenty of water or isotonic drinks beforehand and afterwards.

- When it comes to bondage with open-ended ropes or straps, don't wrap anything around the throat, and don't use slip-knots. Pass the ropes or straps behind the neck and over the shoulders, or use a bondage or pet collar, which will have a pre-determined fastening tighter than which it will not go, and which is far more psychologically loaded anyway.

- If you experiment with gags, and enjoy the extra dimension of surrender that being unable to speak creates, establish a visual expression—it could be batting your eyelashes—that represents a visual safe-word as clearly as possible. Do not gag a partner for long—long-term denial of easy speech and breathing is pleasant only as a fantasy. Remember that breathing and heart-rate will increase with excitement, and sinuses can become blocked. Some gags—such as "O" rings, wiffle-balls, and dental clamps, will create any desired sense of speechless submission without obstructing breathing.

- In keeping with the golden rule above, always test equipment on yourself first, until you know when enough is enough. "Found" bondage and SM objects such as clothespins and wooden spoons can be far more painful than their homey image suggests. Far better to invest in something custom-made, which was designed with an eye to how it would feel, if you can. Use purpose-made bondage tape rather than household tape or duct tape, which will pull body hairs painfully and ruin clothes.

● Ceiling mounts for lighting, along with shower attachments, are not strong enough to support bondage, even with the submissive's feet on the floor. Suspension bondage—where one partner is off the ground—is dangerous; it requires physiological expertise and is best left to those who practice SM like it's a martial art. If you want to get the next-best feeling, invest in a sling and a frame that will support your whole body evenly from beneath.

● The ritualized quality of SM and bondage is utterly compatible with practicing safe sex. Use ribbed or black condoms if you'd like a change.

● Never rush off after kinky sex, even—or rather, especially—if the scenario itself has involved taking each other quickly. Sub-dom sex especially can touch the deepest parts of both participants, and a cuddle is essential. If the submissive has been bound or beaten, they will be bodily aware of that for some time to come—so continue to make sure that their pain has pleasant associations.

● Be aware that some things are more painful than they look. But be aware too that sometimes the bruises and markings of bondage can look more painful and extreme than they feel. Rubbing rope marks and punished areas can be a loving and tender come-down from kinky lovemaking, but you may in fact break further tiny blood capillaries under the skin, delaying their disappearance. Soft kisses will communicate your tender feelings just as well if not better.

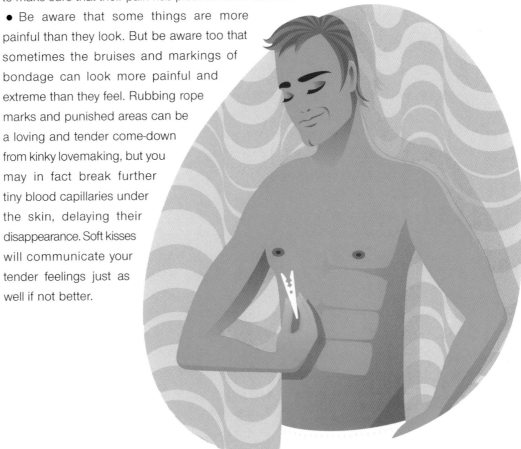

knotty issues
—the tips and tricks of rope bondage

If you want to tie each other up with rope, cord, or scarves, then take note of these fun and essential points.

- Although these materials pull tightly and yet liquidly and comfortably around the human body and limbs, tighten them slowly. Rope, in particular, can cause what used to be referred to as "Chinese burns."

- Scarves make a delicious introduction to the restraint of limbs. They can be tied in wide, comfortable bands that won't intimidate the bondage neophyte.

- Make knots as easy to release as they are to tie.

- Knots can be used both ways—for pain and pleasure. Pay close attention to their positioning to avoid unwanted discomfort. Think also about how their position could be used to stimulate genitals or muscles.

- If it's rope in particular you're interested in playing with, it may help to know that some prefer wound rope of ⅜ in (8 mm) in diameter. Nylon rope is best left to people who go sailing.

- The ideal length for each piece of rope is around 2 ft (60 cm) for wrists or ankles and around 2.5 m (8 ft) for more elaborate constructions around the torso or limbs. To avoid fraying, tie small pieces of cotton thread around the ends.

- Fold each piece of rope in half and mark its middle point with a marker pen. This gives you an easy starting point that you can position in the middle of the span of flesh you're going to bind. As you bind, lay each wrapping of rope alongside the last, creating a wide area of bondage that will not cut the skin as much as one or two wrappings on their own would.

- Keep knots simple—butterfly knots (of the kind with which we tie our shoelaces) are fine unless you get elaborate enough to want to join more than two rope-ends! Use a knot that releases quickly with one easy pull.

- Take care not to draw rope tightly across arteries, creating an accidental tourniquet that restricts blood-flow, or in between skeletal joints.

- If you're experimenting with breast or chest bondage, the submissive should take a deep breath first! Then their lungs will still be able to expand fully when their pulse is racing.

safe sex and loving

Even if you both know you each have a clean bill of sexual health, there's no excuse not to use a condom. The following tips will help you avoid that dreaded moment when the flow of your lovemaking stops as you wrestle with the foil wrapper! Maintain the eroticism between you, and show a bit of style!

A brief genital massage (see pages 54–55) will put him in a mood in which he's likely to maintain an erection. Focusing on his penis as part of your lovemaking will indulge him, turning the condom experience into a treat, not an obligation. Maintain the flow of the massage as you apply the condom. You will tear the latex if you rip the wrapper open with your teeth, so avoid the temptation.

Holding it by the teat at the end to make sure the air is squeezed out, and that it is about to roll in the correct direction down his shaft, rest it on the tip of his penis and roll it down to the base with the other. Don't move straight to placing yourself where he can penetrate you, and don't be hurt if he wants to adjust the condom himself so that his foreskin contracts comfortably, and it remains covering his shaft right to the base.

If condoms are part of your means of avoiding pregnancy and infection, always check the expiry date and use one that conforms to a Federal standard. Novelty condoms aren't designed for contraception or protection, anal sex requires an extra-safe brand.

For a slutty sense of adventure, try putting the condom on with your mouth. A flavored condom will make the experience more pleasant for you, and for him if you're planning on kissing him afterwards! Remove lip-balm, lipstick, or lip-gloss which may contain oils that weaken latex.

Cover your teeth with your lips at all times. Hold the teat of the condom between your pursed lips, sucking inwards lightly to hold it in place. Holding his penis in one closed hand, use your lips to place the condom on its tip. Use your spare hand as necessary to help it down over his glans, and thereafter use your lips and tongue to slide it down the rest of his shaft—a surprisingly deep and sudden feeling for him. Abandon it if and when you can't accommodate any more of him at the back of your throat, and let your hands take over.

index